WORKING DRAWINGS HANDBOOK

WORKING DRAWINGS HANDBOOK

Fourth Edition

Keith Styles and Andrew Bichard

AMSTERDAM • BOSTON • HEIDELBERG • LONDON • NEW YORK • OXFORD
PARIS • SAN DIEGO • SAN FRANCISCO • SINGAPORE • SYDNEY • TOKYO

Architectural Press is an imprint of Elsevier

Architectural
Press

Architectural Press is an imprint of Elsevier
Linacre House, Jordan Hill, Oxford OX2 8DP, UK
30 Corporate Drive, Suite 400, Burlington, MA 01803, USA

First edition 1982
Second edition 1986
Third edition 1995
Reprinted 1998, 2000, 2002, 2003
Fourth edition 2004
Reprinted 2005, 2008

British Library Cataloguing in Publication Data
A catalogue record for this book is available from the British Library

Library of Congress Cataloging-in-Publication Data
A catalog record for this book is available from the Library of Congress

ISBN: 978-0-7506-6372-4

For information on all Architectural Press publications
visit our website at www.architecturalpress.com

Printed and bound in *China*

08 09 10 12 11 10 9 8 7 6 5

Working together to grow
libraries in developing countries

www.elsevier.com | www.bookaid.org | www.sabre.org

ELSEVIER   BOOK AID
International   Sabre Foundation

Contents

Introduction

This book had its origins in the series of articles of the same name published in the *Architects' Journal* in 1976 and 1977. My thanks are due therefore to my fellow contributors to that series, Patricia Tutt, Chris Daltry and David Crawshaw, for many stimulating discussions during its production, and to the *Architects' Journal* for allowing me to reproduce material from it. The text of the first edition, however, was completely rewritten, and responsibility for the views expressed and recommendations made therein were mine alone.

The development of CAD since publication of the third edition has led to a major revision and up-dating to include details of the application of the latest CAD techniques to the whole field of production drawings. This has led to the introduction as collaborator of Andrew Bichard, the well-known architect and writer on CAD topics, who is an acknowledged leader in the field. He has written the sections on CAD, and in particular all the CAD drawings have been produced by him.

It had been hoped at the outset to illustrate the book with actual drawings taken from live projects, but for various reasons this proved to be impracticable. Invariably the scale was wrong, or the drawing was too big, or was too profusely covered with detail irrelevant to the immediate purpose. In the event the drawings in the book have been drawn for it especially, or have been redrawn for it from source material provided by others. My thanks for providing such material are due to Messrs Oscar Garry and Partners, the Department of Health and Social Security, Messrs Kenchington Little and Partners, Autodesk Ltd and the Property Services Agency. Thanks are also due to The British Standards Institution, The Royal Institute of British Architects, and the Construction Project Information Committee for permission to use material for which they hold the copyright.

A final caveat: the illustrations have been selected – indeed, in many instances devised – solely for their function in illustrating points made in the text, and are not presented as working details to be used for any other purpose.

The structure of information

No one who has delivered drawings to site and overhead the foreman's jocular reference to a 'fresh set of comics having arrived' will deny that the quality of architects' working drawings in general is capable of improvement. In some measure we have all of us suffered more or less justifiable accusations of inaccuracy, inadequacy and incomprehensibility; and yet drawings are prepared and issued with the best of intentions. Few offices deliberately skimp the job, despite economic pressures and time constraints, for the consequences of inadequate or incorrect information being passed to the builder loom frighteningly behind every contract. We do our genuine best, and still things go wrong which might have been avoided; still information is found to be missing, or vague, or incorrect (**1.1**).

The UK Building Research Establishment paper 'Working Drawings in use' lists a depressing number of defects which the authors found giving rise to site queries. Those defects included:

- uncoordinated drawings—(i.e. information from different sources found to be in conflict)
- errors—items of information incorrect
- failures in transmission—(i.e. information produced and available but not put in the right hands)

- omissions—items of information accidentally missing
- poor presentation—(i.e. the drawing or set of drawings was complete but confusing to read).

Analysis of this list suggests that the defects spring from different causes—some from an inadequate understanding of the user's needs, some from an undisciplined approach to the problems of presenting a complex package of information, and some from faulty project management procedures. That the problems seem to arise more frequently in relation to architects' drawings than to those of other disciplines merely illustrates how the difficulty is compounded by the complicated nature of the architect's work and the diversity of the information they have to provide. The structural engineer need only adopt a simple cross-referencing system to enable him to link any structural member back to a general arrangement drawing; but for an architect economically to give precise and simply understood directions about, say, a door set—involving a range of variables which include door, frame, architrave, finishes, materials and ironmongery—a communications method of some complexity will be required. Where is such a method to be found (**1.2**)?

1.1 *Hellman's view of the problem*

Problems of communication

The *Handbook of Architectural Practice and Management* (published by the Royal Institute of British Architects) points out, 'As with all technical communication, the user's needs are the primary consideration'. Whoever the user is—and the users of a set of drawings will be many and various—he has the right to expect that the information given to him will be:

- an accurate record of the designer's intentions
- clearly expressed and easily understood
- comprehensive and sufficiently detailed for its purpose
- easily retrievable from the mass of other information with which, inevitably, it will be combined.

It is the purpose of this book to consider these four requirements in detail and hopefully to propose techniques for satisfying them.

There is a fifth and fundamental requirement, of course. The information conveyed must be technically sound; if this is not the case then all the careful draughting and

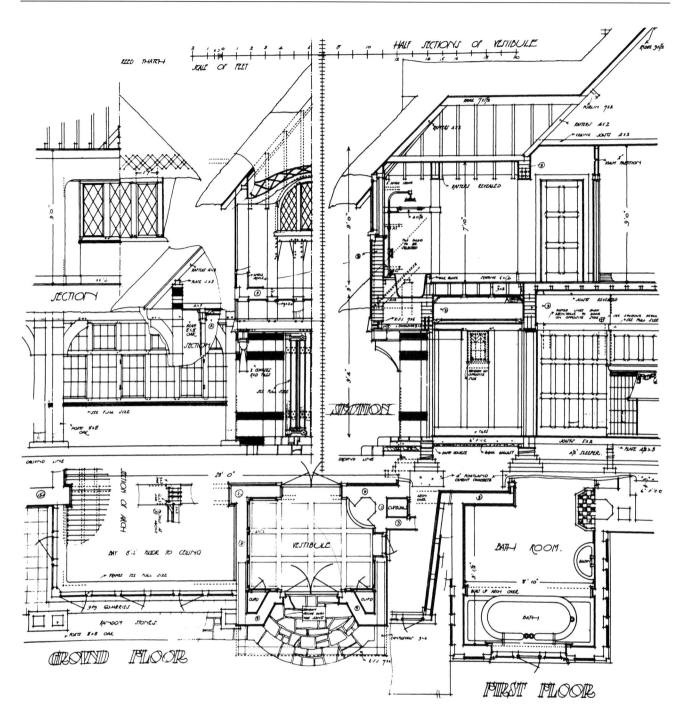

1.2 *House at Gerrards Cross by A. Jessop Hardwick, c. 1905. A typical working drawing of its era, in both its draughting techniques and its obsessive use of every inch of the drawing sheet (RIBA Drawings Collection)*

cross-referencing will not be sufficient to prevent disaster. This aspect, however, lies outside the scope of the present book which must concern itself only with the adequate documentation of technical decisions made at an earlier stage. In RIBA Plan of Work terminology, the decisions belong to stage E; their documentation belongs to stage F.

The plan of work

Since what we shall be looking at is in effect a series of disciplines, and since the plan of work is the overriding discipline into which the working drawing process is integrated, it is probably worthwhile reminding ourselves of it at the outset. Table I of the outline plan of work is given here in its entirety.

Frequent reference to the plan of work will be made in this book, for it is important that stage F production drawings should be seen in the context of the whole architectural process, forming the vital link between the designer's intention and the builder's execution of it. The successful implementation of many of the techniques to be dealt with here will depend upon proper procedures having been carried out at earlier stages, whilst the whole *raison d' être* of the drawing set lies in the stages following its production.

The users

There are many users of a set of drawings and each may put it to more than one use. Unless the set is to be redrawn expensively to suit the ideal requirements of each, priorities must be established and compromises accepted. Consider the following functions of a set of drawings (the list is by no means exhaustive).

It forms for different people and at different times:

- a basis for tendering ('bidding' in USA)
- a contractual commitment

- a source for the preparation of other documents
- a statement of intent for the purpose of obtaining statutory consents
- a framework for establishing nominated sub-contractors or suppliers
- a source for the preparation of shop drawings
- a shopping list for the ordering of materials
- a construction manual
- a model for developing the construction programme
- a supervising document
- a record of variations from the contract
- a base document for measurement of the completed works and preparation of the final accounts
- a base document for defects liability inspection
- a record of the completed structure
- a source of feedback.

It will be noted that the majority of these uses involve the contractor and clearly his needs are paramount, if only for the purely legal reason that it is he who will be contractually committed to the employer to build what the architect tells him to. They may be separated into three main activities and any drawing method must satisfy all three if it is to prove viable.

Activity 1: The procurement of all necessary materials and components. For this the contractor will need the following information in a form in which it can be identified readily and extracted for ordering purposes:

A specification of the materials to be used, which can be referred back simply to the drawings and the bills of quantities.

Drawings and schedules of all components which he is to provide (doors, windows, etc.) and which constitute measured items in the bills of quantities.

Drawings and schedules from which outside manufacturers' products may be ordered and which provide design criteria against which manufacturers' shop drawings may be checked.

Table I The RIBA Plan of Work

Feasibility	**A**	**Appraisal**
		Identification of client's requirements and of possible constraints on development. Preparation of studies to enable the client to decide whether to proceed and to select the probable procurement method.
	B	**Strategic Briefing**
		Preparation of Strategic Brief by or on behalf of the client confirming key requirements and constraints. Identification of procedures, organisational structure and range of consultants and others to be engaged for the project.
Pre-construction period	**C**	**Outline Proposals**
		Commence development of Strategic Brief into full Project Brief.
		Preparation of Outline Proposals and estimate of cost.
		Review of procurement route.
	D	**Detailed Proposals**
		Complete development of the Project Brief.
		Preparation of Detailed Proposals.
		Application for full Development Control approval.
	E	**Final Proposals**
		Preparation of Final Proposals for the project sufficient for coordination of all components and elements of the project.
	F	**Production Information**
		F1 Preparation of production information in sufficient detail to enable a tender or tenders to be obtained. Application for statutory approvals.
		F2 Preparation of further production information required under the building contract.
	G	**Tender documentation**
		Preparation and collation of tender documentation in sufficient detail to enable a tender or tenders to be obtained for the construction of the project.
	H	**Tender Action**
		Identification and evaluation of potential contractors and/or specialists for the construction of the project. Obtaining and appraising tenders and submission of recommendations to the client.
Construction period	**J**	**Mobilisation**
		Letting the building contract, appointing the contractor.
		Issuing of production information to the contractor. Arranging site hand-over to the contractor.
	K	**Construction to Practical Completion**
		Administration of the building contract up to and including practical completion.
		Provision to the contractor of further information as and when reasonably required.
	L	**After Practical Completion**
		Administration of the building contract after practical completion.
		Making final inspections and settling the final account.

The Work Stages into which the process of designing building projects and administering building contracts may be divided. (*Some variations to the Work Stages apply for design and build procurement.*)

Published by RIBA 1998. By permission of RIBA

Activity 2: The deployment of plant and labour. For this he will need:

> Drawings showing the extent of each trade's involvement.
>
> A 'construction manual' describing, by means of annotated drawings, the way in which each trade is to operate and which is explicit enough to ensure that no local querying or decision-making will be necessary.
>
> An objective and realistic description of the quality standards required and the methods to be employed.

Activity 3: The preparation of a programme and decision on a method of operation. For this he will need:

> Drawings giving an overall picture of his commitment.
>
> Comprehensive information about the constraints of site, access and programme.
>
> A summary of his contractual obligations.

The need for a unified system

What we are looking for is a complete information system which will satisfy these different user requirements and which will be at the same time:

- reasonably simple and economical to produce
- simple to understand and to use at all levels
- flexible enough to embrace information produced by various offices—structural, M & E, etc.
- capable of application to both small and large projects
- appropriate for use in both small and large producing offices.

The importance of the two latter points tends to be underestimated. Given a standard method of procedure a common experience is gradually built up, not only among contractors but among assistants moving from one project to another within the office, or indeed moving between different offices. Nothing is more disruptive for architect, estimator and contract manager alike than to have to switch constantly from one working method to another.

It was with this in mind that the Project Information Group (commonly known by its somewhat unfortunate acronym) was set up to identify more precisely the reasons for the inadequacies in building information previously noted.

In the course of time the Group became transmuted into the Construction Project Information Committee, upon which the main building professional and contracting organisations are represented and which in 2003 published a sequence of Co-ordinated Project Information (CPI) documents. These represent what is to date the most comprehensive statement of intent regarding the achievement of better production information.

Among other aspects they acknowledge the concept of drawings, specifications and bills of quantities, together forming the complete information package, and despite the existence of ingenious alternative methods which have been devised for particular situations it is not the intention of this book to disturb that long-standing tripartite relationship.

Consideration will be given in a later chapter to what information sometimes given on drawings may be more appropriate to the specification; but other than that this book will concern itself solely with drawings, regarding them as the base documents in the information package which it is the role of the specification to amplify, the bills to quantify (**1.3**).

The structure of working drawings

Every set of working drawings consisting of more than one sheet is structured, for it represents a more or

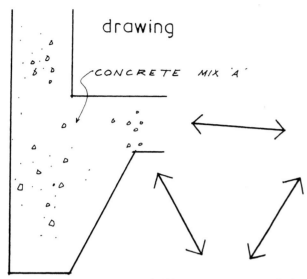

drawing

CONCRETE MIX 'A'

specification

and, in the case of fine aggregates, Zones 1 to 3 only sh
The maximum size of coarse aggregate shall not be less th
otherwise specified.

Aggregates shall comply with B.S. 882 and shall be fre
elongated particles, dust, clay films and other adherent
shall not contain clay lumps exceeding 1% by weight and f
shall not contain more than 3% by weight of silt.

In addition to the above it is required that the aggre
not produce a drying shrinkage in any of the concrete use

Methods of storage must be such as to ensure freedom f
intermingling and segregation. In general, separate coar

bills of quantities

C	Foundation in trench, over 300 mm thick.	16	m^3
D	Extra over for placing around live drain.	1	m
E	Ditto, in pit, over 300 mm thick	5	m^3
F	Casing to steel beam, over 0.05 and not exceeding 0.10 m^2 sectional area.	2	m^3
G	Ditto, not exceeding 0.05 m^2 sectional area.	1	m^3
H	Casing to steel column, over 0.05 and not exceeding 0.10 m^2 sectional area.	1	m^3
J	Ditto, not exceeding 0.05 m^2 sectional		

1.3   *Drawings, specification and bills of quantities. Each has a clearly defined role in the building package*

less conscious decision on the part of the draughtsman to put certain information on one sheet of paper and certain other information on others. Even were the reason for doing so simply that there is insufficient space on a single sheet of paper, a selection has still to be made of what to put on each sheet and a sensible basis for that division has to be determined.

Indeed, the simplest of single sheet applications to a local authority for approval under the Building

Regulations for the erection of a garage is likely to contain a small-scale plan showing the site in relation to the surrounding neighbourhood as well as a dimensioned plan of the building itself. This in effect acknowledges the existence of some informational hierarchy within which certain different aspects of instruction about the building may sensibly be given in different places and in different ways (**1.4**).

In the following pages we shall be not so much seeking to impose a method of doing this as seeking out the

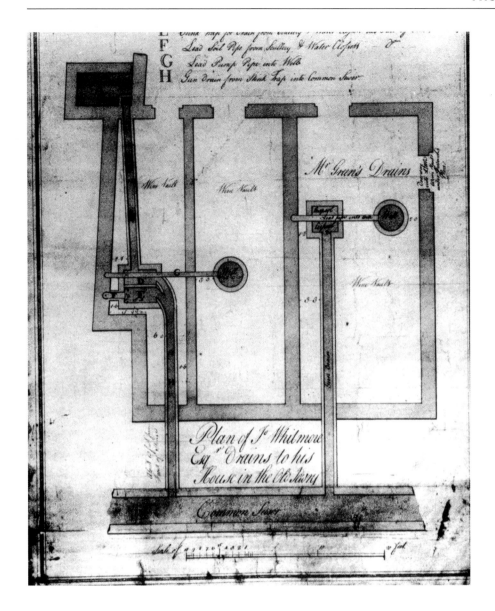

1.4 *Detail from an early example of elementalisation. Drainage plan by James Adam, c.1775 (RIBA Drawing Collection)*

structure inherent in the whole concept of building information, and trying to reflect it in the form that the information package will take.

Let us start our search at the point where the ultimate end product of the entire communications exercise is to be found—the building site.

What, where and how?

The information that an operative needs to know about each element of the building he is called upon to construct may be classified into three distinct types:

1   He needs to know *what* it is that he has to install or erect. Whether it be a window frame, brick or cubic

metre of concrete, he needs to know certain information about its nature and physical dimensions.

2 He needs to know *where* it is to be placed. This demands pictorial and dimensional information regarding its relationship to the building as a whole.

3 He needs to know *how* it is to be placed or fixed in relation to its immediate neighbouring elements.

Clearly, these three questions—*what, where* and *how*—are fundamental to the business of building communications, and demand a variety of replies in practice if they are to be answered satisfactorily and without ambiguity. It may be useful to reflect for a moment on the degree of depth and comprehensiveness that may be required of these answers.

If the designer has devised a precise solution to the building problem set him by his client, then the information to be conveyed to the builder must be of sufficient detail to enable the unique nature of that solution to be appreciated and converted into physical building terms by a variety of people, most of whom will be unfamiliar with the original problem and unaware of the chain of thought processes which has given rise to its solution.

So if we are dealing with a window, the single question—What window?—may proliferate into a large and varied series: what are its overall dimensions; what does it look like; what material is it made from; what is its glass thickness; what furniture does it have; what are its finishes? These and many other questions will arise from consideration of the nature of a single component.

Similarly we need to know where in the building it is to be installed, implying the need for dimensional information in three planes; and how it is to be installed—how it sits in relation to the lintel above it, how it relates to the vertical DPCs in the adjacent wall cavities, how many fixing points are required and what is the nature of their fixing. And so on.

The amount of information required so that the description of any aspect of the building will be unambiguous must always be a matter for intelligent consideration. The strength and density of bricks forming footings below ground level, for instance, will be fit subjects for precise description, whereas their colour will not.

But two fundamental principles emerge which will be found to hold good at all times.

1 All building information may be classified into three basic categories, depending upon which of the three basic questions—how, where and what—it purports to answer.

2 All building information is hierarchic in its nature and proceeds from the general to the particular.

This latter observation requires some discussion, because the sequence in which the three questions which were posed at the start of this section emerge may suggest that the seeker after information starts with the component and its nature and then works outwards to a consideration of where and how to install it. This sequence is in fact occasionally true—the window manufacturer, for example, would tend to consider the type of window he was being called upon to make before determining how many of them were in the building and how they were distributed throughout it.

But in general terms the reverse is true. Almost every user of the information package will wish to know that there is a wall of finite dimensions with windows in it which forms the outer boundary of the building, before seeking to determine the various forms that the windows might take or the precise nature of the bricks and their pointing.

Since this is also the manner in which the designer will logically work, there is little difficulty, and every advantage, in devising a system in which the search for information starts with the question Where? The answer to this question indicates where the answers may be found to the supplementary questions What? and How?

Primary structuring—by information type

What has been outlined is a method of primary structuring of information according to its type, and which may be summarised and named as follows:

- *Location* information, answering the questions: where are components to be built or installed and where further information about them may be found?

- *Component* information, answering the question: what is the component like?
- *Assembly* information, answering the question: how are the various components to be related one to another—how are they to be assembled?

This type of structure and the search pattern it generates is illustrated in (**1.5**). It is to be noted that the CPI recommendations adopt a similar method of classification, the only difference being that location

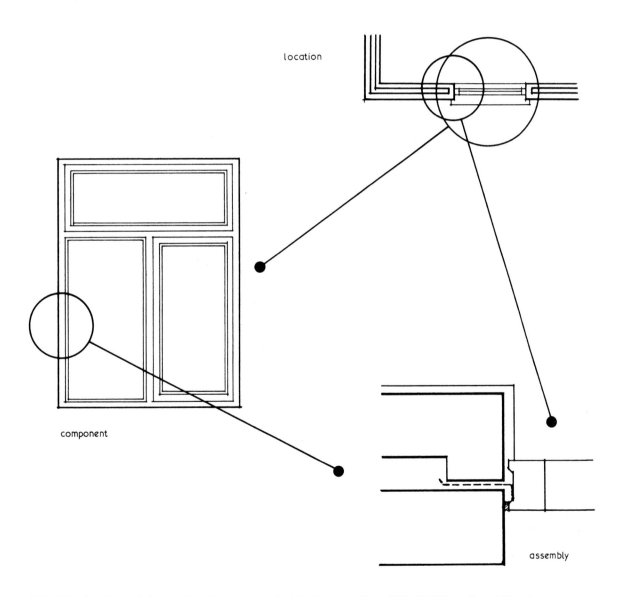

1.5 *The fundamental search pattern generated by the questions What?, Where? and How?*

drawings are termed 'general arrangement drawings'. The term 'location drawing' has long been established within the architectural profession and the mnemonic SLAC (schedule, location, assembly, component) is in common use. Nevertheless, it seems likely that the CPI terminology will become increasingly known and used. The term 'general arrangement' has in any case long been used in the engineering disciplines and has therefore been used throughout the remainder of this book.

Into this neatly classified system must now be introduced that somewhat hybrid creature, the schedule. It must be made clear at the outset that the term 'schedule' here referred to is confined to basic lists of information—primarily about components—which are more readily set out in this manner than on the drawings. (The Schedule of Works, as envisaged in the CPI documents for smaller projects, has a different function, more akin to the bills of quantities.)

The idea of using written schedules, or lists of information, exists in most information systems and has its source in a variety of motives, not all of them necessarily valid. It is assumed that they are economical of drawing office time; that quantity surveyors, contractors and suppliers alike all welcome them; and that they provide a ready check that the information conveyed is comprehensive.

These reasons do not always stand up to close examination. Schedules are only economical if they are simpler than the drawings they replace; the architect should not necessarily be doing other people's jobs for them; suppliers more often than not produce their own schedules because the architect's schedule is not in a form which they find usable; and some schedules attempt to provide so much information in so complicated a form that mistakes and omissions readily occur.

Nevertheless, they have a role to play and used sensibly and with forethought they form an essential element in the information package.

Some principles affecting scheduling

> Their primary function is to identify and list components possessing common characteristics—e.g. windows, doors, manhole covers, etc.
>
> They should not attempt to provide comprehensive information about the component; they should serve rather as an index to where the relevant information may be found.
>
> They should initiate a simple search pattern for the retrieval of component, sub-component and assembly information.
>
> They are only worth providing if the component in question has more than one variable. For instance, if you have windows of three different sizes which are identical in every other respect, then size is the only variable and you may as well write 'Window Type 1' on the general arrangement plan as 'Window no. 1'. But if each window size may be fixed into either a brick wall or a pre-cast concrete panel then the assembly information required is a second variable.
>
> Window Type 1 may be combined with jamb detail type 1 or type 2, and it is for this greater degree of complexity that it is preferable to prepare a schedule.

The great virtue of the schedule is that it can direct you to a vast amount of information about a given component in a way that would be impossible by any system of direct referencing from a general arrangement drawing. Consider a window—thirty-seventh, shall we say, of fifty-one on the second floor of a multi-storey block of offices. The method chosen for giving it a unique reference is unimportant for the moment—W2/37 is as good a piece of shorthand as any for the purpose—but it is obvious that this simple means of identification may be shown equally on a drawing or a schedule (**1.6**).

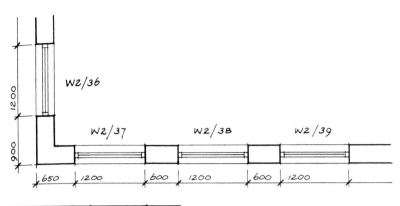

1.6 *Simple identification of components may be recorded on either a schedule or general arrangement plan*

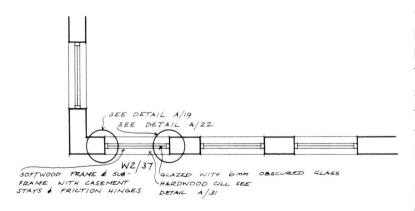

1.7 *The general arrangement plan is an inappropriate medium for recording the diverse characteristics of each component. Detail of this order can only be given elsewhere—in a specification or in other drawings to which the schedule points the way*

Thus, there are two ways of providing a catalogue of the windows on the job, in which W2/37 is seen to take its place between W2/36 and W2/38. But if we were now to add to the drawing a fuller description of what W2/37 in fact consists of, then we should meet an immediate difficulty—there is just not space to do it (**1.7**).

Consequently, when it is considered that the information given only scratches the surface of what the recipient really needs to know and that similar information will need to be provided about W2/1 to W2/50—to name but the windows on the second floor—it becomes apparent that not only will there be insufficient room on the drawing to make this method feasible but there will be insufficient drawing office time and money available to make it an economic starter. The schedule does it so much better (**1.8**).

Given the presence of schedules in the package, the search pattern given in (**1.5**) becomes simpler and more directly focused. The general arrangement drawing is still the starting point but now the searcher is directed from it to the schedule and from there to the various sources of assembly and component information (**1.9**).

Further consideration will be given later to the most suitable format for schedules and to the areas of information which lend themselves most readily to scheduling. All that remains to be settled for the moment is what sort of an animal this hybrid most resembles. Is it a drawing or some other form of document? If a drawing, then what type of drawing is it?

window no.	window type	width	height	component detail no.	l.h. jamb detail no.	r.h. jamb detail no.	cill detail no.	head detail no.	etc.
W2/36	WA	1200	1800	C/15	A/19	A/22	A/31	A/36	
W2/37	WB	1200	2100	C/19	A/19	A/22	A/31	A/42	
W2/38	WA	1200	1800	C/15	A/19	A/22	A/31	A/36	
W2/39	WC	1200	2400	C/20	A/17	A/18	A/30	A/37	

1.8 *The schedule provides a simple and economical index to a variety of information*

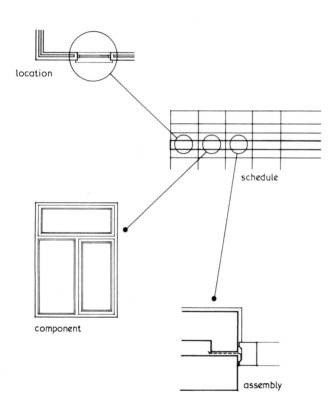

location

schedule

component

assembly

1.9 *The fundamental search pattern of **1.5** now runs through the schedule*

In practice it does not really matter provided that all the implications of your choice have been fully considered and that having made your decision you are consistent in sticking to it.

The schedule's function is primarily that of an index and as such it will at different times direct the searcher towards assembly drawing, general arrangement drawing, specification, trade literature and, possibly, the bills of quantities. If considered as a drawing then it clearly possesses all the directive qualities of a general arrangement drawing. But it will inevitably be of a different nature—and indeed size—from the other general arrangement drawings in the package, and its status as such puts it in an anomalous situation when used in conjunction with other documents—as an adjunct to the bills of quantities, for example.

Maximum flexibility in use is therefore achieved by acknowledging the hybrid nature of the schedule for what it is and by treating it as an independent form of document in its own right, capable equally of being bound into a set of drawings or into a specification.

The package is nearly complete. However, it requires two further categories of drawing to render it entirely comprehensive. They may be dealt with quite quickly.

Sub-component drawings: First, it will become desirable at times to illustrate how a component itself is made. The frame sections of a timber window, for example, are often better shown separately from the drawing showing the window itself, for they may well be applicable to a number of windows whose overall sizes and appearances are widely different. Yet to term the drawing

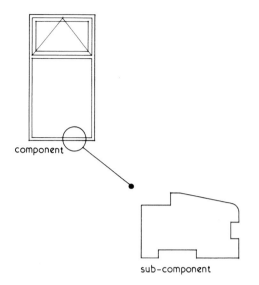

1.10 *The sub-component drawing illustrates how the component itself is made*

showing these sections a 'component drawing' is inaccurate, as well as being potentially confusing. In the hierarchy of information it is clearly one step lower and more detailed.

It is, in fact, a sub-component drawing and there is a place for it as such in the set (**1.10**).

Information drawings: Second, there is a class of drawing which conveys information, not so much about the building and its elements as about the building's background. Such matters as the site survey, records of adjoining buildings, light envelope diagrams, bore hole analyses, all fall into this category. They have this feature in common, which distinguishes them from the other drawings in the package, that they convey information without giving instructions (**1.11**). (It should be noted that a cross-section of the building such as is shown in (**3.16**) in Chapter 3, and condemned there as conveying little constructional direction to the builder, might nevertheless form a useful information drawing for anyone planning a building programme.)

The complete primary structure: The complete primary structure is summarised in (**1.12**). It is worth noting that this complete drawing package, which has to be all things to all men, is now capable of sub-division into smaller packages, each of which is tailored to suit the needs of the individual recipient. The bricklayer needs to know the position and size of the window he has to install, but has no interest in the manner in which it is made in the joiner's shop. Similarly, the local authority will not require the complete set of drawings for approval (even though the extravagant demands of certain Building Control officers in this respect may induce in frustrated practitioners a somewhat cynical smile at this statement).

With occasional exceptions, however, the drawing set may be used as shown here, with attendant advantages of order and economy. The focal position of the schedule is well demonstrated.

Secondary structuring

The good old-fashioned working drawing floor plan—ancestor of the general arrangement plan and aimed at embracing every piece of information necessary for the erection of the building—still survives in places but its defects are now so generally recognised that it is possibly unnecessary to spend much time in demonstrating them. Figure **1.13**, taken almost at random from such a drawing, shows the disadvantages.

The sheet is cluttered with information, making it extremely difficult to read. The notes and references fill every available corner, and in an attempt to crowd too much information into too small a compass the draughtsman has had to resort to a lettering style of microscopic dimensions. Any alteration to it would be difficult both to achieve and to identify. (Figure **1.2** also illustrates the defects inherent in the 'one drawing' approach.)

This is a case of one drawing attempting to do the work of several, and simplicity, legibility and common sense

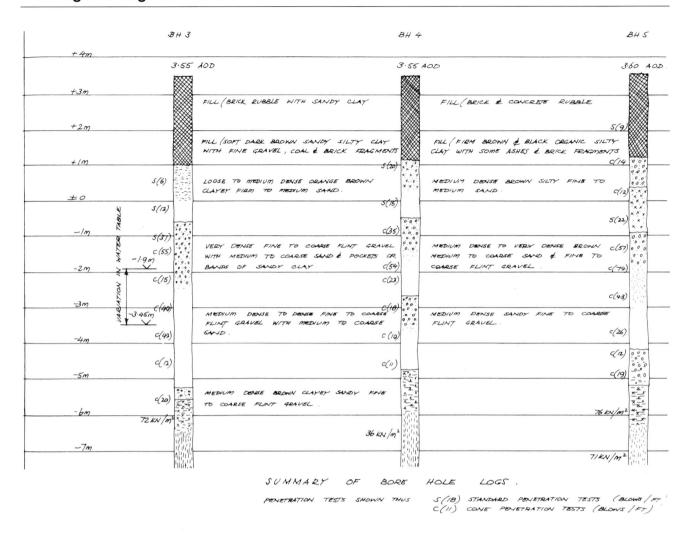

BH 3   BH 4   BH 5

3·55 AOD   3·55 AOD   3.60 AOD

FILL / BRICK RUBBLE WITH SANDY CLAY   FILL / BRICK & CONCRETE RUBBLE
                                                                             S(9)
FILL / SOFT DARK BROWN SANDY SILTY CLAY   FILL / FIRM BROWN & BLACK ORGANIC SILTY
WITH FINE GRAVEL, COAL & BRICK FRAGMENTS   CLAY WITH SOME ASHES & BRICK FRAGMENTS
                                        S(20)   C(14)
S(6)   LOOSE TO MEDIUM DENSE ORANGE BROWN   MEDIUM DENSE BROWN SILTY FINE TO
       CLAYEY FIRM TO MEDIUM SAND.   MEDIUM SAND.   C(12)
                                        S(16)
S(12)   S(22)
                                        C(35)
S(37) VERY DENSE FINE TO COARSE FLINT GRAVEL MEDIUM DENSE TO VERY DENSE BROWN C(57)
C(55) WITH MEDIUM TO COARSE SAND & POCKETS OR MEDIUM TO COARSE SAND & FINE TO
       BANDS OF SANDY CLAY   C(54) COARSE FLINT GRAVEL.   C(74)
C(15)   C(23)
                                                                             C(43)
C(40)   C(18) MEDIUM DENSE SANDY FINE TO COARSE
       MEDIUM DENSE TO DENSE FINE TO COARSE   FLINT GRAVEL.
       FLINT GRAVEL WITH MEDIUM TO COARSE
C(43) SAND.   C(10)   C(12)
                                        C(11)   C(19)
C(20) MEDIUM DENSE BROWN CLAYEY SANDY FINE
       TO COARSE FLINT GRAVEL.   76 kN/m²
72 kN/m²
                                               36 kN/m²   71 kN/m²

VARIATION IN WATER TABLE
−1·9m
−3·45m

SUMMARY OF BORE HOLE LOGS.

PENETRATION TESTS SHOWN THUS   S(18) STANDARD PENETRATION TESTS (BLOWS/FT)
                               C(11) CONE PENETRATION TESTS (BLOWS/FT)

1.11 *Typical information drawing—this record of bore hole findings provides the contractor with useful background information but gives no instructions about the building*

would all be better served if there were several drawings to replace it. Let us consider the various ways in which the crowded information might be distributed.

The Department of the Environment Report, 'Structuring Project Information' lists no fewer than nine separate non-traditional systems that include in their make-up some degree of information structuring. The 1970s and 1980s saw a widespread and largely uncoordinated experimentation in building communications techniques, generated by an increasing demand on the resources of an overstretched profession and building industry, and a growing awareness of the inefficiency and waste of time on building sites being caused by inadequate documentation. Not all these systems were at that time sufficiently well tested to allow a genuine evaluation of their merits.

Now, some twenty years later, we are in a better position to obtain a proper perspective of the field, and the problem becomes somewhat clearer. Some of the communications systems then presenting themselves for

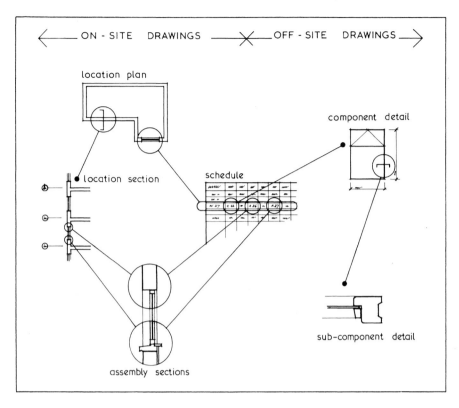

1.12 *The complete primary structure of building drawings information*

consideration are now seen to be so closely associated with the requirements of specific organisations or constructional systems that they lack universal applicability. Others, reliant upon a more radical refashioning of the bills of quantities than is envisaged here, offer possible pointers to the future and are discussed later.

All accept the primary structuring of drawn information represented in this book by the general arrangement/ assembly/component format. Where they tend to diverge is in their approach to secondary structuring and their methods of identifying and coding it.

The building operation and indeed the completed building, may be considered in a number of ways. You may regard it, for example, as an assemblage of different materials. To some extent the specification does just that, describing with precision the type of sand, the type of cement and the size of aggregate to be used, as well as describing their admixture into concrete (the point at which the bills of quantities take an interest).

You may look at it, on the other hand, as a series of different trade activities, in which case you would tend to regard as one package of information all work done by the carpenter and as another package all work done by the plumber. Bills of quantities have traditionally been structured on these lines, the concept lying at the heart of the Standard Method of Measurement. It has been one of the primary tasks of the Construction Project Information Committee in its development of the Common Arrangement of Work Sections to seek out a rational method of terminology for building operations that would be acceptable to all the building disciplines.

In drawing terms, however, neither the materials-based nor the activity-based sub-division relates very happily to the architectural realities. To the quantity surveyor one cubic metre of concrete may be very like another but when one forms part of the foundations and another part of the roof slab, it is over-simplistic to suggest that both should form part of a series of 'concrete' or 'concretor' drawings.

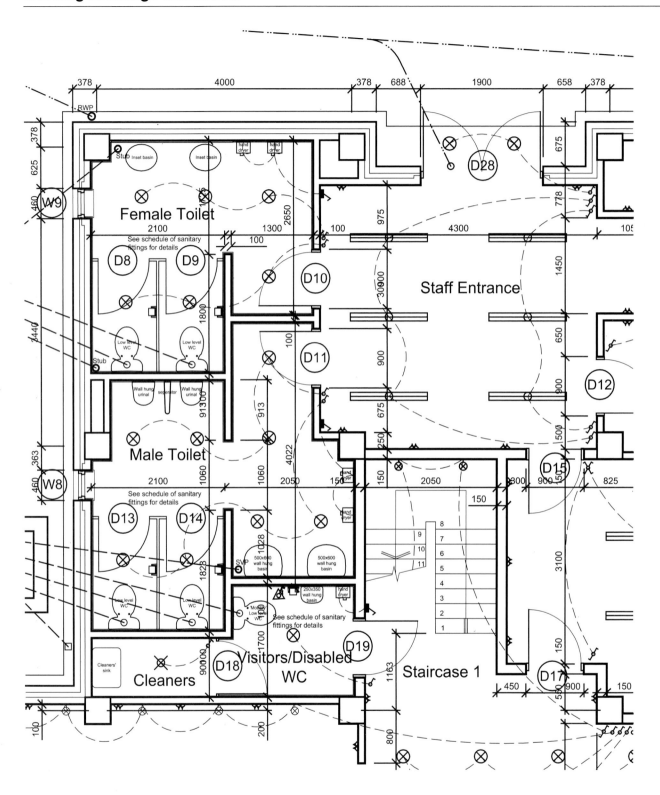

1.13 *Drawing attempting to show everything ends up by showing nothing very clearly (original scale 1:50)*

Drawings are by definition concerned with the perceived form of the building and if we are to sub-divide them then a breakdown into the different elements of their form is more logical than an attempt to classify them by either material or trade sub-divisions. (A criticism that may be levelled at the Uniclass Table G—Elements for buildings—is that it is too much oriented towards materials and procedures; a defect that is largely avoided in the simpler provisions of CI/SfB Table I).

Both systems of classification co-exist in the profession at the present time and are dealt with later in this chapter.

In the meantime let us return to the cluttered example shown in (**1.13**) and separate it into three elements chosen at random, collecting information about the walls on one drawing, floor finishes on another and the doors on a third (**1.14**, **1.15** and **1.16**).

At once we can see what we are doing. The notes and references to other drawings are relatively few and sparsely distributed, so that they catch the eye, and plenty of space is left for further annotation should this become desirable during the course of the project. Furthermore, to anyone who knows how this particular set of drawings is sub-divided the search pattern for any aspect of the building is straightforward. If someone wants to know about windows they can go straight to the general arrangement drawing dealing with windows, from which point the search pattern described previously can proceed within the narrow confines of window information. The general search pattern, shown diagrammatically in (**1.17**) now follows a series of paths, each related to a specific aspect of the building (**1.18**).

The advantages of this are two-fold. In the first place the designer now has a framework upon which to display his information; in the second place the user has an authoritative guide through the informational labyrinth.

It should be noted that the drawings illustrating this have been prepared using CAD. In most offices the decision on whether small drawings such as these are drawn by hand or by computer will hinge, as here, on the complexity, longevity and distribution of the information to be conveyed, and the number of CAD seats available in the office. In practice, the illustrations shown here, while small in themselves, show part of a much larger complex and the question of drawing them manually never really arose.

Structuring by building element

Within the framework of a primary structuring by information type, the information to be shown is sub-divided by building element and this constitutes the secondary structuring of the drawing set.

To establish the possible means of achieving this we should start by looking at the various ways in which the building fabric may be regarded. Consider the diagram in (**1.19**).

It is difficult to visualise any space-enclosing structure, no matter how primitive, which does not possess elements falling within one or other of the four categories shown. A little thought, however, will suggest that this is an oversimplification, and that a minimal sub-division of elements would look much more like (**1.20**). The elements here have one common feature—they are all structural. We may introduce other elements but it is apparent that then we are setting up another hierarchy of information analogous to the hierarchy established when considering types of information (**1.21**).

Coding the set

It is one thing to recognise the existence of this hierarchy and another thing altogether to set it down in simple and universally acceptable terms. The trouble with hierarchic systems—in building communications as

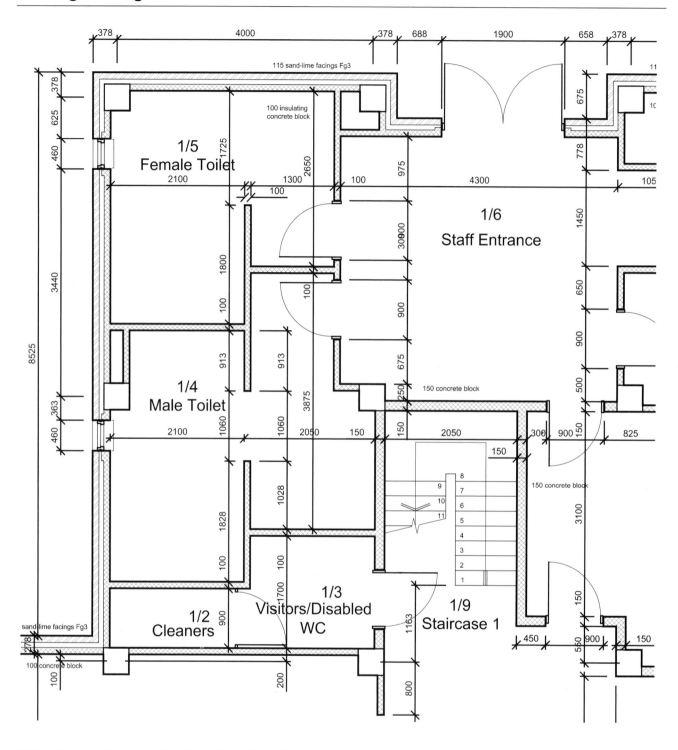

1.14 *Elemental version of **1.13** dealing with walls—(21)*

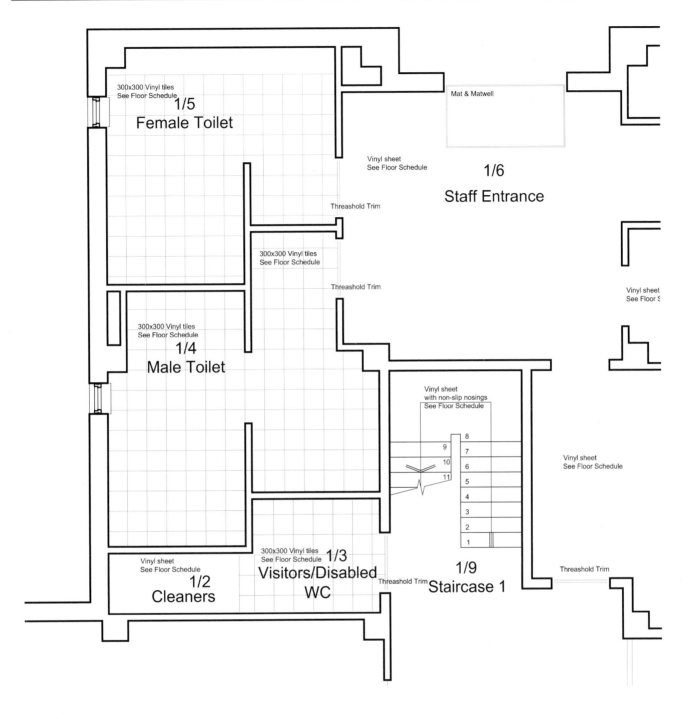

1.15 *Elemental version of 1.13 dealing with floor finishes—(43)*

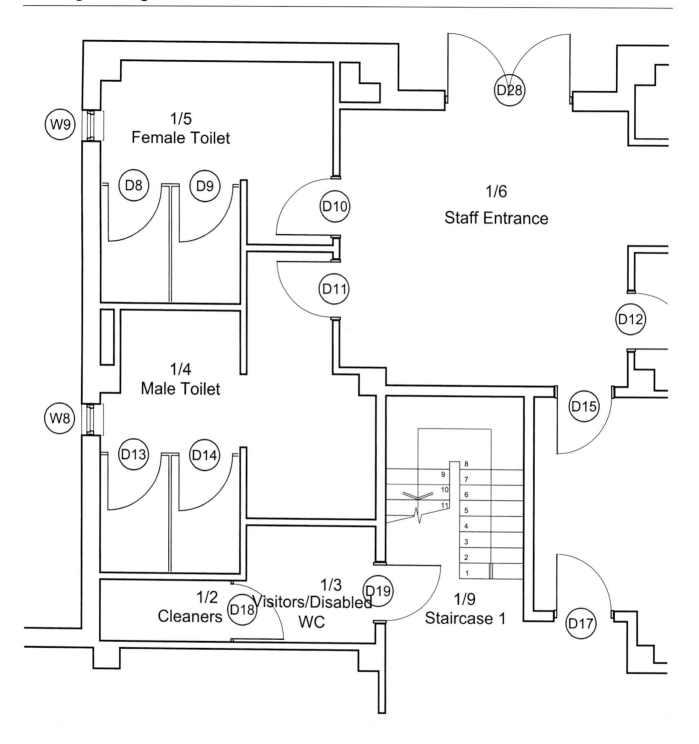

1.16 *Elemental version of 1.13 dealing with doors and windows—(31)*

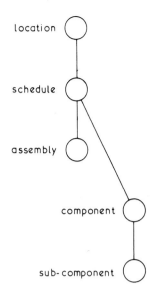

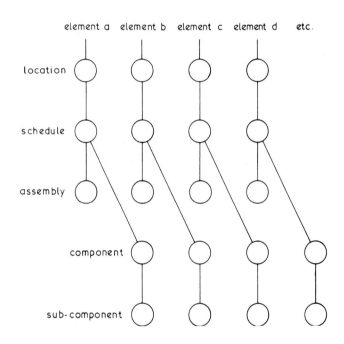

1.17   *The fundamental search pattern*

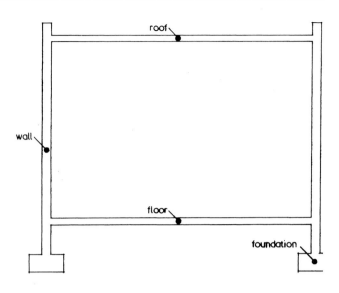

1.19   *The simplest possible division of building structure*

1.18   *Search pattern running through different building elements*

1.20   *Sub-division of building into structural elements*

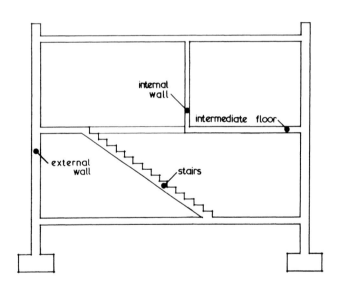

in politics—is that they tend to be complex, difficult to understand and self-defeating when applied too rigidly. Their great advantage—in building communications at any rate—is that they offer the user access at the level

most appropriate to his purpose. So we are looking for a method of elementalising the building which fulfils the following requirements:

• It should be simple to understand
• It should be universally applicable

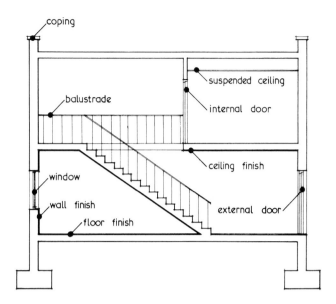

1.21 *Further sub-division of the fabric leads to increasing complexity*

• It should operate on a number of levels, permitting greater or less sub-division of information depending upon the size and complexity of the building in question.

Home-made systems

It is not difficult to devise your own systems to meet these requirements. Indeed, in practice many offices do, varying the method each time to suit the complexity of the job in hand. Within the primary general arrangement/assembly/component framework, for instance, it is possible to divide the drawings on a small project into, say, brickwork (series B), windows (series W), doors (series D), etc. The precise method of sub-division and of coding is of less importance than recognising the existence of an inherent primary and secondary structure.

There are two generally accepted methods, however, which despite certain defects will, if adopted, fulfil most of the requirements enumerated above.

Uniclass Table G

This is the system set out in the 2003 CPI Code of Procedure, and as such has the advantage of being consistent in its terminology with the Common Arrangement of Work Sections. (The National Building Specification operates under the Common Arrangement.)

Having said that, it should be pointed out that the Uniclass headings relate to building elements, while the Common Arrangement is specifically materials-oriented. Uniclass Table G (Table II) is an attempt to reconcile these divergent objectives, but in essence is simply a tabulation and naming of the elements forming the secondary structure of a set of drawings.

You will note that the table is broken down into the following primary elements:

G1 Site preparation
G2 Fabric: complete elements
G3 Fabric: parts of elements
G4 Fittings/furniture/equipment (FFE)
G5 Services: complete elements
G6 Services: parts of elements
G7 External/site works

These generic headings clearly require sub-division if they are to be of use in coding the drawings. Consequently, there is a second level of headings, of which the 57 main sub-headings are broken down into further sub-divisions. To take two instances at random:

G251 External walls is seen to break down into:

G311 Core fabric
G312 Coverings/external finishes to external walls
G321 External windows
G322 External doors
G333 Internal finishes to external walls

Table II Uniclass Table G

Elements for buildings G

G1 Site preparation	G11	Site clearance	
	G12	Ground contouring	
	G13	Stabilisation	
G2 Fabric: complete elements	G21	:G311 Foundations (foundations consist entirely of core fabric)	
	G22	Floors	
	G221	Lowest floors	:G311 Core fabric
			:G331 Floor finish to lowest floors
			1 Direct
			2 Raised floor
	G222	Upper floors	:G311 Core fabric
			:G331 Floor finish to upper floors
			1 Direct
			2 Raised floor
			:G332 Ceilings/soffit finishes to upper floors
			1 Direct
			2 Suspended
	G23	Stairs	Balustrades are at G251 and G252. However, if preferred, balustrades to stairs/ramps may be included here.
			:G311 Core fabric
			:G33 Stair finish
			11 Top
			21 Soffit
	G24 Roofs		:G311 Core fabric
			:G312 Roof coverings
			:G321 Roof lights
			:G332 Roof soffit finishes/ceilings to roofs
			1 Direct
			2 Suspended
			:G34 Roof edges
			Includes parapets, gutters, etc. Rainwater downpipes are at G5812.
			:G25 Walls
	G251 External walls		Includes external balustrades.
			:G311 Core fabric
			:G312 Coverings/external finishes to external walls
			:G321 External windows

Table II   (continued)

Elements for buildings G

		:G322	External doors
		:G333	Internal finish to external walls
	G252 Internal walls and partitions	Includes internal balustrades.	
		:G311	Core fabric
		:G321	Internal windows
		:G322	Internal doors
		:G333	Internal finish to internal walls
	G26 Frame/isolated structural members	:G311	Core fabric
		:G334	Frame finish
			Where separate from ceiling and wall finishes.
G3 Fabric: parts of elements		G31	Carcass/structure/fabric
	G311 Core fabric	:G21	Foundations (foundations consist entirely of core fabric)
		:G221	Core fabric of lowest floors
		:G222	Core fabric of upper floors
		:G23	Core fabric of stairs
		:G24	Core fabric of roofs
		:G251	Core fabric of external walls
		:G252	Core fabric of internal walls
		:G26	Core fabric of frame
	G312 Coverings/external finishes	:G24	Coverings of roofs
		:G251	Coverings/external finishes to external walls
		G32	Openings
	G321 Windows	:G24	Roof lights
		:G251	External windows
		:G252	Internal windows
	G322 Doors	:G251	External doors
		:G252	Internal doors
		G33	Internal finishes
	G331 Floor finishes	1 Floor finishes, direct	
		:G221	To lowest floors
		:G222	To upper floors
		:G23	To stairs
		2 Floor finishes, raised	
		:G221	To lowest floors
		:G222	To upper floors
	G332 Ceilings/soffit finishes	1 Ceilings/soffit finishes, direct	
		:G222	To upper floors
		:G23	To stairs
		:G24	To roofs
		2 Ceilings/soffit finishes, suspended	

Table II   (continued)

Elements for buildings G

		:G222	To upper floors
		:G24	To roofs
	G333 Wall internal finishes	:G251	To external walls
		:G252	To internal walls
	G334 Other internal finishes	:G26	Frame finishes Where separate from ceiling and wall finishes.
	G34 Other parts of fabric elements	:G24	Roof edges Includes parapets, gutters, etc. Rainwater downpipes are at G5812.
G4 Fittings/furniture/ equipment (FFE)	G41 Circulation FFE		
	G42 Rest, work FFE		
	G43 Culinary FFE		
	G44 Sanitary, hygiene FFE		
	G45 Cleaning, maintenance FFE		
	G46 Storage, screening FFE		
	G47 Works of art, soft furnishings		1 Works of art 2 Soft furnishings
	G48 Special activity FFE		Classify with reference to Table D Facilities.
	G49 Other FFE		

G5 Services: complete
elements
	G50 Water supply		For mains water supply see G751.
			Classify parts with reference to
			Section G6, e.g.:
			G50:G61 Energy generation/
			storage/conversion for water supply
			G50:502:G632 Pipework for water
			supply
			G502:G632 Pipework for hot
			water supply
			1 Cold water
			2 Hot water
			9 for special activity
			   Classify with reference to
			   Table D Facilities.

	G51 Gas supply		For mains gas supply see G754. Classify parts with reference to Section G6, e.g.: G51:G632 Pipework for gas supply
	G52 Heating/ventilation/air conditioning (HVAC)		Classify parts with reference to Section G6, e.g.: G52:G61 Energy generation/ storage/conversion for HVAC

Table II   (continued)

Elements for buildings G

		G52:G631 Ductwork for HVAC
		1 Heating
		2 Heating + non-cooling air conditioning
		3 Heating + cooling air conditioning
		4 Ventilation
		1 Supply and extract ventilation
		2 Extract ventilation
		For smoke extraction/control see G5723
		9 For special activity
		Classify with reference to
		Table D Facilities, e.g.:
		G529:D73 Special HVAC
		services for laboratories
	G53 Electric power	For electric mains see G755.
		Classify parts with reference to
		Section G6, e.g.:
		G53:G61 Energy generation/
		storage/conversion for electric power
		1 General purpose outlets
		2 Supply to service installations
		9 For special activity
		Classify with reference to
		Table D Facilities.
	G54 Lighting	For outdoor lighting see G761.
		Classify parts with reference to
		Section G6.
		1 General lighting
		2 Emergency lighting
		9 For special activity
		Classify with reference to
		Table D Facilities
	G55 Communications	Classify parts with reference to
		Section G6
		1 Public address
		2 Visual display
		3 Radio
		4 TV
		5 Telephones
		6 Computer networks
		9 For special activity
		Classify with reference to
		Table D Facilities, e.g.:
		G559:D 14 Special
		communications services for air transport

Table II (continued)

Elements for buildings G

	G56 Transport	Classify parts with references to Section G6.
		1 Lifts/hoists
		2 Escalators
		3 Conveyors
		4 Travelling cradles
		9 For special activity
		Classify with reference to Table D Facilities, e.g.:
		G569:D284 Special transport services for industrial warehouses (including mechanical handling systems)
	G57 Protection	Classify parts with reference to Section G6.
		1 Security
		1 Entrance controls
		2 Intruder/security alarms
		2 Fire
		1 Fire/smoke alarms
		2 Fire fighting and sprinkler installations
		3 Smoke extraction/control installations
		3 Other protection
		1 Lightning protection
		9 For special activity
		Classify with reference to Table D Facilities.
	G58 Removal/disposal	Classify parts with reference to Section G6.
		1 Drainage
		1 Foul drainage
		2 Surface water drainage
		Includes rainwater downpipes. Gutters are at G24:G34.
		2 Refuse disposal
		9 For special activity
		Classify with reference to Table D Facilities.
	G59 Other services elements	
G6 Services: parts of elements		For mains supply see G75. Classify sound attenuation for services elements with the appropriate part in the list below.

Table II   (continued)

Elements for buildings G

		For example classify sound attenuation for distribution elements at G63.
	G61 Energy generation/storage/ conversion	Classify the complete elements to which these parts belong with reference to Section G5, e.g.:
		G61:G50 Energy generation/ storage/conversion for water supply
		G61:G52 Energy generation/ storage/conversion for HVAC
		G61:G53 Energy generation/ storage/conversion for electric power
		1 Heat output
		1 Heat generation
		i.e. boilers (including fuel storage), solar collectors.
		2 Heat conversion
		i.e. calorifiers, heat exchangers,
		2 Electricity output
		1 Electricity generation
		i.e generators, turbines, photovoltaic cells.
		2 Electricity conversion
		i.e. transformers, convertors.
		3 Cooling output
		4 Combined heat/power/cooling
	G62 Non-energy treatment/ storage	Classify the complete elements to which these parts belong with reference to Section G5.
	G63 Distribution	Classify the complete elements to which these parts belong with reference to Section G5, e.g.:
		G631:G52 Ductwork for HVAC
		G632:G50 Pipework for water supply
		G632:G51 Pipework for gas supply
		1 Ductwork
		2 Pipework
		3 Cables
		4 Pumps
		5 Fans
	G64 Terminals	Classify the complete elements to which these parts belong with reference to Section G5.

Table II   (continued)

Elements for buildings G

	G65 Package units	Classify the complete elements to which these parts belong with reference to Section G5.
	G66 Monitoring and control	Classify the complete elements to which these parts belong with reference to Section G5.
	G69 Other parts of services elements	
G7 External/site works	G71 Surface treatment	1 Hard surfaces
		2 Landscaping
	G72 Enclosure/division	1 Fencing/walling/hedges
		2 Retaining walls
	G73 Special purpose works	1 Water features, pools
		2 Shelters, minor buildings
		3 Bridges, underpasses
		9 Other
	G74 Fittings/furniture/equipment	
	G75 Mains supply	1 Water mains
		2 Fire mains
		3 Hot water/steam mains
		4 Gas mains
		5 Electric mains
		6 Communications cable mains
	G76 External distributed services	1 Lighting
		2 Other
	G77 Site/underground drainage	

In this table the combined codes under each main element have been abbreviated for the sake of clarity of presentation. For example, at G24 Roofs, the entry ':G312 Roof coverings' is an abbreviation for 'G24:G312 Roof coverings'.

The full codes should be used when quoting Uniclass codes.

G252 Internal walls and partitions is seen to break down into:

| G311 Core fabric |
| G321 Internal windows |
| G322 Internal doors |
| G333 Internal finishes to internal walls |

Clearly, the Uniclass system, in endeavouring to embrace the conflicting needs of draughtsman, specifier and quantity surveyor, renders its use for the classification of drawings unnecessarily complex. It will no doubt be modified in the future, as its defects become tested in practice and found wanting. At the moment however it is possible to rationalise our approach to it:

1   The only possible justification for structuring a set of drawings is that it makes life easier for everybody to do so. The moment this ceases to be the case (and it would have to be a pretty small project for this to happen) the system becomes self-defeating and you would be better off without it.

2 When we talk of elementalising the drawings we are in effect talking almost exclusively of the general arrangement drawings. These are the only drawings which will be drawn elementally in the sense that the same floor plan, for example, may be shown several times—either by CAD or manually—to illustrate the various elements contained within it. All other categories of drawing—assembly, component, sub-component, schedule—may well fall within one or other of the elemental sub-divisions; but they will be drawn uniquely and will appear only once in the drawing set.

3 Although all the facets of Uniclass Table G are available, like so many pigeon-holes, to receive the various drawings prepared, there is no particular virtue in trying to use them all. In practice a very few will suffice, even for the larger projects. Never forget the two-fold objective of this secondary structuring, which is to provide both a disciplined framework for the draughtsman and a simple retrieval method for the seeker after information. A drawing set containing a couple of drawings in each of some thirty elemental sub-divisions assists the achievement of neither.

4 Given a true understanding of the objectives common sense is the paramount consideration.

With this in mind Table G might well be simplified into:

G1 Site preparation
G21 Foundations
G22 Floors
G24 Roofs
G25 Walls
G26 Frame
G32 Openings
G33 Internal finishes
G4 Fittings/furniture/equipment
G5 Services
G52 Heating/ventilation/air conditioning
G54 Lighting
G7 External works.

Such a division will probably be adequate for coding all but the very largest and most complicated projects. If it should be found desirable however to deal separately with, for example, doors and windows, the further sub-divisions G321 and G322 are available.

CI/SfB

An alternative method is in existence which fulfils most of the requirements of an elemental structuring system and which has the advantage of being already well established within both the profession and the industry. This is the CI/SfB method of classification, and while it has its detractors, who legitimately point to certain weaknesses in detail, it has so many advantages in logic and flexibility that on balance it must be recommended. The CPI documents accept it as a viable alternative to Uniclass Table G, and consequently it will form the basis of most of the drawings illustrated in subsequent chapters.

Its virtues are:

- It is currently the most widely known and used of available classification methods.
- It is comprehensive in its scope, offering opportunities for uniting the output of different disciplines into a common package.
- It is capable of operation at various levels of sophistication, making it suitable for both large and small projects.
- It is fully compatible with the Co-ordinated Project Information elementalised concept.
- It is compatible with the use of computer-aided draughting.

The complete CI/SfB system is undoubtedly complex (though considerably less so than Uniclass Table G), and some tend to shy away from it, frightened at the prospect of having such a sophisticated sledge-hammer to crack such small nuts as are the mainstay of the average practice. This is a pity, for that aspect of CI/SfB which is of greatest relevance to the drawing office is in fact of a disarming simplicity. (It is certainly less

Table III CI/SfB Table 1

(—) Project in general

(1—) Substructure, ground	(2—) Primary elements	(3—) Secondary elements	(4—) Finishes	(5—) Services piped, ducted	(6—) Services, electrical	(7—) Fittings	(8—) Loose furniture equipment	(9—) External, other elements
(10)	(20)	(30)	(40)	(50)	(60)	(70)	(80)	(90) External works
(11) Ground	(21) Walls, external walls	(31) External wall openings	(41) Wall finishes, external	(51)	(61) Electrical	(71) Circulation fittings	(81) Circulation, loose equipment	(91)
(12)	(22) Internal walls, partitions	(32) Internal wall openings	(42) Wall finishes, internal	(52) Waste disposal, drainage	(62) Power	(72) Rest, work fittings	(82) Rest, work loose equipment	(92)
(13) Floor beds	(23) Floors, galleries	(33) Floor openings	(43) Floor finishes	(53) Liquids supply	(63) Lighting	(73) Culinary fittings	(83) Culinary loose equipment	(93)
(14)	(24) Stairs, ramps	(34) Balustrades	(44) Stair finishes	(54) Gases supply	(64) Communications	(74) Sanitary, hygiene fittings	(84) Sanitary, hygiene loose equipment	(94)
(15)	(25)	(35) Suspended ceilings	(45) Ceiling finishes	(55) Space cooling	(65)	(75) Cleaning, maintenance fittings	(85) Cleaning, maintenance loose equipment	(95)
(16) Retaining walls, foundations	(26)	(36)	(46)	(56) Space heating	(66) Transport	(76) Storage, screening fittings	(86) Storage, screening loose equipment	(96)
(17) Pile foundations	(27) Roofs	(37) Roof openings	(47) Roof finishes	(57) Air-conditioning, ventilation	(67)	(77) Special activity fittings	(87) Special activity loose equipment	(97)
(18) Other substructure elements	(28) Building frames, other primary elements	(38) Other secondary elements	(48) Other finishes to structure	(58) Other piped, ducted services	(68) Security, control, other services	(78) Other fittings	(88) Other equipment	(98) Other elements
(19) Parts of (11) to (19), cost summary	(29) Parts of (21) to (29), cost summary	(39) Parts of (31) to (39), cost summary	(49) Parts of (41) to (49), cost summary	(59) Parts of (51) to (59), cost summary	(69) Parts of (61) to (69), cost summary	(79) Parts of (71) to (79), cost summary	(89) Parts of (81) to (89), cost summary	(99) Parts of (91) to (99), cost summary

complicated than some home-made systems one has encountered over the years.)

Before looking at this aspect in detail, however, let us look briefly and without going into superfluous detail, at the whole range of the CI/SfB system of classification. There are five tables in the complete CI/SfB matrix:

Table 0 deals with building types and its codes are always of the nature B1.

Table 2 deals primarily with manufactured components. Typical examples would be blockwork—blocks (code F), tubes and pipes (code I), or thin coatings (code V). The codes are always as shown, consisting of a single upper case letter.

Table 3 deals with basic materials, such as clay, dried fired (code g2), gypsum (code r2), or flame-retardant materials (code u4). It will be seen that when used with the codes of Table 2 they provide a method of shorthand for quite specific descriptions of components—such as blocks in lightweight aggregate Fp3, clay tiles Ng2, or plywood Ri4.

Table 4 deals with the various techniques involved in the physical process of building, such as testing (Aq) or demolition (D2).

In terms of classification for drawing purposes however, we need consider only Table 1 dealing with building elements—stairs, roofs, ceiling finishes, etc.

The codes are always bracketed, in the form (24), (27), (45), etc.

CI/SfB Table 1 is here given in its entirety (Table III):

The hierarchic structure is immediately apparent. Within it each building element may be considered at any of three levels, the level selected being determined by the complexity of the project in question and the need to break down the conveyed information into categories of a manageable size. Any element within the building—a lavatory basin, for example—may clearly be regarded as forming part of 'The project in general (—)'. But it may also be considered as coming within the category of 'Fittings (7-)' (the seventh of the main sections into which the table is divided). Finally, it may be regarded as coming within the quite specific grouping of 'Sanitary, hygiene fittings (74)', the fourth sub-division of section (7-).

Windows, in similar fashion, may be seen as coming within the (—), (3-) or (31) headings, terrazzo flooring as (—), (4-) or (43). And so on.

The primary and secondary information structure is therefore complete and we are ready to move on to detailed consideration of what each drawing should contain and what it should attempt to convey to the recipient.

The general arrangement drawing

The types of drawing which make up the complete set having now been identified, the following two chapters look at them in sequence to see the sort of information that each should contain. A brief reference must be made here, however, to the means of producing them.

There are two methods:

1 Drawing them manually, by means of ink or pencil on tracing paper. Until relatively recently this was the only available method.
2 Drawing them electronically on a computer screen using a mouse and printing the result. This is Computer-Aided Draughting which has so many advantages that it is now in almost universal use in all but the smallest architects' offices.

Both techniques are dealt with in detail in Chapter 4. It is worth noting here, however, that the basic principles of elementalising and organising the drawing set are virtually identical for each method.

The general arrangement drawing

The drawings falling into this category will normally include:

- floor plans at all levels
- reflected ceiling plan at all levels
- roof plan
- foundation plan
- external elevations
- general sections and/or sectional elevations
- site plan.

Floor plans

There are three situations to consider:

- General arrangement (location) drawing designed to show a single building element and what it should contain.
- The general arrangement drawing designed to be complete in itself—i.e. a drawing which in CI/SfB Table 1 terminology would be described as

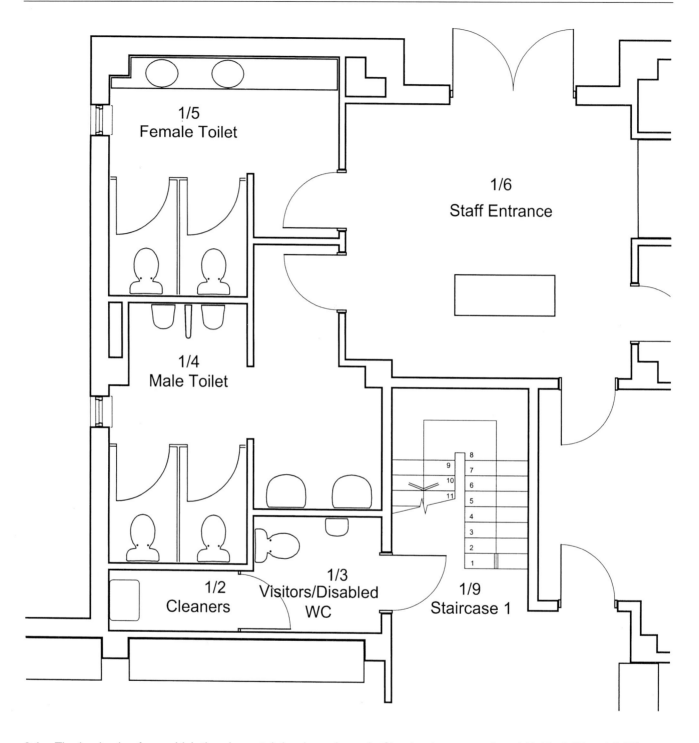

2.1 *The basic plan from which the elemental drawings shown in Chapter 1 were produced (**1.14**, **1.15** and **1.16**)*

'The project in general' and coded (--). (Clearly this type of drawing would only arise on the smallest and simplest of projects.)

- The basic general arrangement drawing—the drawing which provides the fundamental and minimal information which will appear as the framework for each individual elemental plan. The basic drawing, in fact, from which future drawings containing elemental information will be taken.

Since the latter has a substantial bearing on the other two, it will be dealt with first.

The basic floor plan   Let us assume that you are to prepare a set of working drawings for a building project and that, by means of techniques to be discussed in a later chapter, you have decided that the floor plans will be divided into five elements in the following manner:

(2-)   Primary elements
(3-)   Secondary elements
(5-)   Services (piped and ducted)
(6-)   Services (Electrical)
(7-)   Fittings.

The basic plan from which these elemental drawings will be produced is shown (produced by CAD) in **2.1**.

General arrangement plans   Whether the elemental plans are to be drawn by CAD or manually, you must first consider what common features of the plan will need to appear in all five elementalised plans. It is clearly important that the information carried by the base negative, (manual) or layers common to all drawings in a CAD set shall be (like the amount of lather specified in the old shaving soap advertisement), not too little, not too much, but just right. See below for a check list of what the basic plan should contain and a list of those

items which more often than not get added to the original needlessly and superfluously, to the subsequent inconvenience of everyone.

To be included:

- Walls
- Main openings in walls (i.e. doors and windows)
- Partitions
- Main openings in partitions (doors)
- Door swings
- Room names and numbers
- Grid references (when applicable)
- Stairs (in outline)
- Fixed furniture (including loose furniture where its disposition in a room is in practice predetermined—e.g. desks set out on a modular grid, etc.)
- Sanitary fittings
- Cupboards
- North point.

Items which tend to be included but should not be:

- Dimensions
- Annotations
- Details of construction—e.g. cavity wall construction
- Hatching or shading
- Loose furniture where its disposition is not predetermined
- Section indications.

The basic plan (**2.1**) gives an idea of what should be aimed at. Note that a uniform line thickness is used throughout and that this is the middle of the three line thicknesses to be recommended in Chapter 4.

The elemental floor plan   Generally speaking, if a project needs to be dealt with elementally then it will need to be separated into most or all of the following:

*(2-) Primary elements (walls, frames, etc.)

(3-) Secondary elements—possibly sub-divided into:

    (31) secondary elements to external walls
        (windows, etc.)

    (32) secondary elements to internal walls (doors, etc.)

    (35) suspended ceilings

(4-) Finishes—possibly sub-divided into:

    (42) internal finishes

    (43) floor finishes

    (45) ceiling finishes

*(5-) Services—possibly sub-divided into any or all of the
    various constituent services

*(6-) Installations—possibly sub-divided into:

    (62) power

    (63) lighting

    (64) communications

(7-) Fittings—possibly sub-divided into:

    (74) sanitary, hygiene fittings (WCs, sinks, basins)

    (76) storage, cleaning fittings (shelving, window
        rails, etc.)

(8-) Loose equipment.

* May well be produced by other than the architect.

In other words, the breakdown is into the primary facets of CI/SfB Table 1, and only in one or two instances is it sometimes necessary to go any deeper. The reasons for this are apparent from a common-sense appraisal of the reason for elementalising the general arrangement floor plan in the first place—the desire to produce simple uncluttered drawings upon which different types of information will not be laid unidentifiably and confusingly one upon the other. If you consider the possible sub-divisions of the primary element facet it will be apparent that any drawn or annotated information about (21) external walls is unlikely to conflict with information about (22) internal walls or (23) floor construction. The different elements are physically separated on the drawing and complete legibility may be maintained even though they share the same sheet of paper. Similarly,

(31) external openings are unlikely to conflict with (32) internal openings and both may appear on the same drawing under the generic coding of (3-).

Refer back to **1.14**, **1.15** and **1.16** in Chapter 1, where the basic plan illustrated in **2.1** has been utilised as the framework for various elemental plans—in this case primary elements, floor finishes and secondary elements.

The project of which these drawings form part was a two million pound office and workshop complex with a reinforced concrete frame. In practice both the reinforced concrete structure and the electrics would have been carried out by other consultants, as in **2.2** and **2.3**.

This project will be used throughout the book to illustrate various aspects of working drawing practice.

Finishes With regard to finishes generally, the practice of laboriously covering the floor plan with descriptive wall, floor and ceiling finishes on a room-by-room basis is not to be recommended. It is impossible for the plan to give detailed enough information without exhaustive (and exhausting) annotation. (See attempt made to convey this information about room 1/9 in **2.4**.) A system of coded reference back to a written schedule is a more practical alternative, as shown in room 1/18 in the same illustration. The references A/7, B/3 and B/2 relate to a vocabulary of finishes given separately in written form, where the repetitive nature of the relatively few types of finish involved makes it possible to record them in detail without too much time-consuming room-by-room annotation.

Non-graphical room-by-room scheduling is a more satisfactory alternative. It is easy to produce and to refer to, and a lot of information may be conveyed by it. It has its disadvantages, the main one being the difficulty of relating the written description to an actual wall area or door surface, but on the whole it is a reasonably effective method (**2.5**).

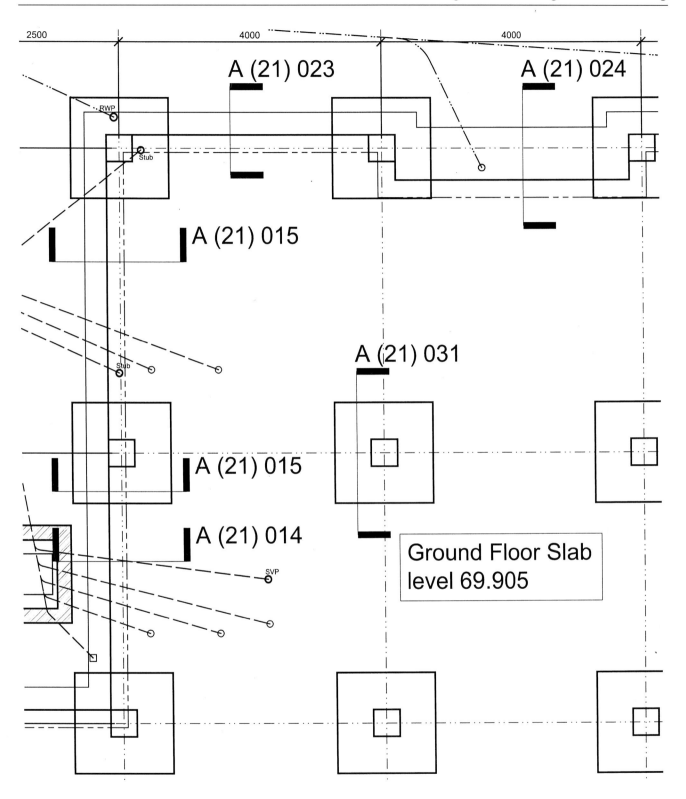

2500   4000   4000

A (21) 023

A (21) 024

RWP

Stub

A (21) 015

Stub

A (21) 031

A (21) 015

A (21) 014

SVP

Ground Floor Slab
level 69.905

2.2 *Elemental structural layout (28) based on* **2.1**

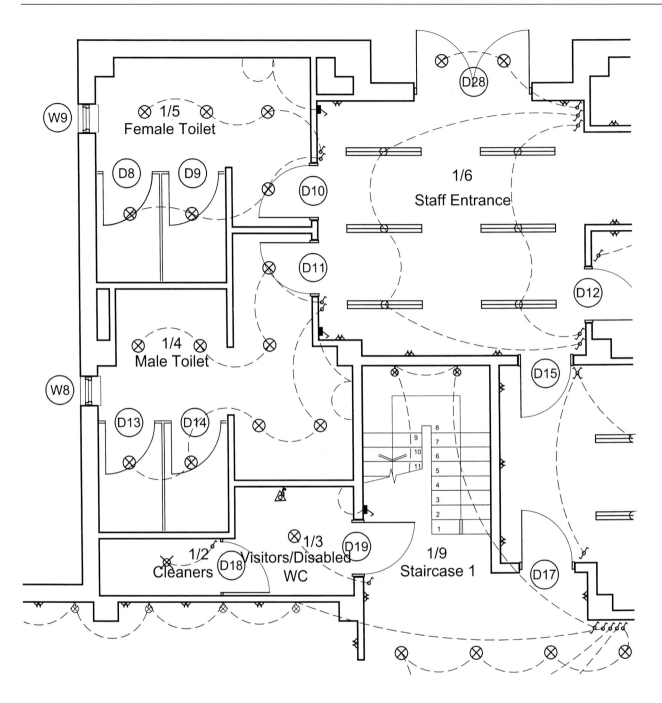

2.3 *Elemental electrical layout—(63) based on **2.1***

Of course, a description such as 'Two coats of emulsion' is helpful only to the estimator. Ultimately somebody is going to ask 'what colour?' and a method of documentation which does not offer facilities for providing

a concise answer (let alone the possibility of explaining that you want the chimney breast in a different colour from the rest of the room) is an ill-considered one. So while there is a case to be made for including in the set a plan

40

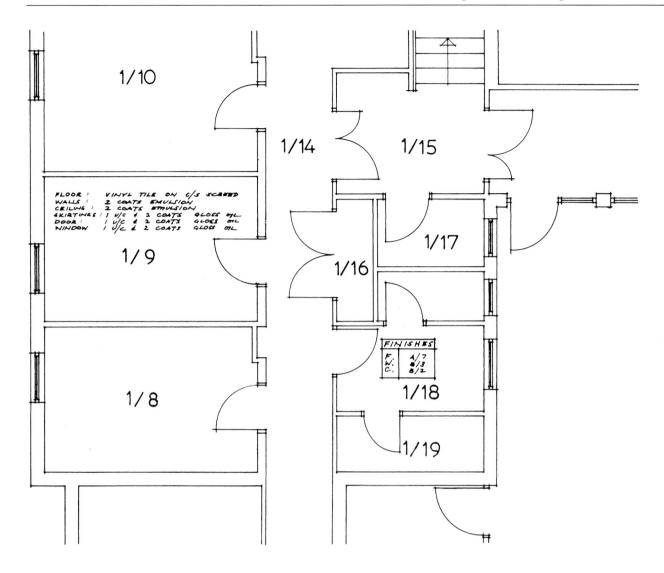

2.4 *Coded system of finishes in room 1/18 compares favourably with over-elaborate annotation of finishes for room 1/9*

coded (43) and dealing solely with floor finishes, which will serve as a base drawing for dealing with nominated suppliers, finishes pertaining to walls and their ancillaries for any room other than the most simply decorated are best dealt with by a series of internal elevation sheets covering the whole project on a room-by-room basis.

Figure **2.6** shows a workable format for this and demonstrates its use in positioning accurately those miscellaneous items which if otherwise uncoordinated are apt to make an unexpected and unwelcome visual impact during a site visit late in the contract.

Specific problems arise when we come to ceilings, services and finishes. Some consideration must be given to the best method of documenting these, for boundaries tend to overlap and clear thinking is essential.

Ceiling Finishes Ceiling finishes complete the room but before simply opting for a (45) coded reflected

ROOM NAME			ROOM NO.
ELEMENT	FINISH	SPEC. CLAUSE NO.	COLOUR
FLOOR			
SKIRTING			
HEATER			
WALLS 1			
WALLS 2			
WALLS 3			
WALLS 4			
COLUMNS			
CILLS			
WINDOWS			
DOORS			
FRAMES			
CEILING			
FITTINGS			

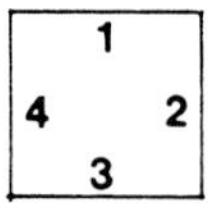

	NOTES	A	
(wall diagram: 1, 4, 2, 3)		B	
		C	
		D	
WALL NOS.		E	

2.5 *Finishes given in schedule form. Strong on descriptive detail, though weak on actual location, it nevertheless offers a simple and effective method*

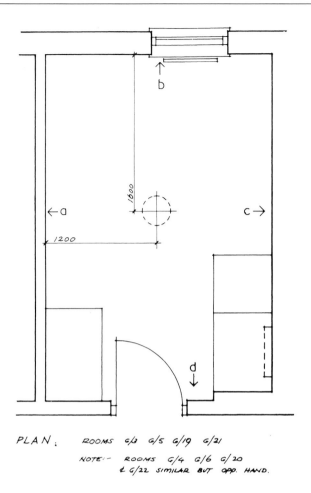

PLAN : ROOMS G/3 G/5 G/19 G/21

NOTE :- ROOMS G/4 G/6 G/20 & G/22 SIMILAR BUT OPP. HAND.

ceiling plan the implications must be considered of any suspended ceilings (which CI/SfB Table 1 would have us code (35)) and of the lighting and air conditioning layouts, both of which will normally have a bearing on the ceilings.

Let us be clear about what we are trying to achieve. There will be a general arrangement plan of air-conditioning trunking—no doubt prepared by the M & E engineer—and coded (assuming other consultants are working within the CI/SfB format), G(57). There will also be a lighting layout, a sprinkler layout, etc. and each will also be a general arrangement drawing of the appropriate coded reference. Should a drawing be produced to consolidate these various services, to ensure that they can co-exist satisfactorily in the same ceiling void, then it might be thought to be an assembly drawing and sensibly coded A(5-), since the services as a whole are its primary concern. But at the end of the day the architect's drawing must be of the ceiling *per se*, so that the precise positioning of diffusers, lighting fittings, sprinkler heads, etc. may be visually acceptable and may be taken to represent the 'picture on the lid' for all concerned with the construction of it. This is in every

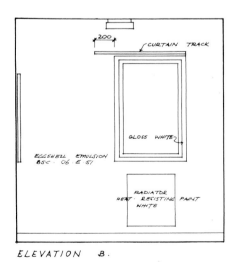

ELEVATION B.

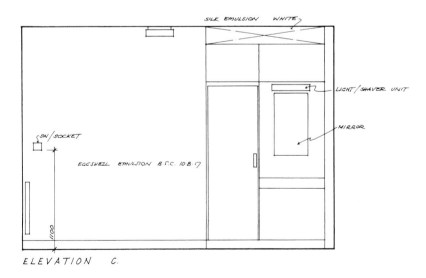

ELEVATION C.

2.6 *Internal elevations on a room-by-room basis is the most flexible method for conveying information on finishes (cont.)*

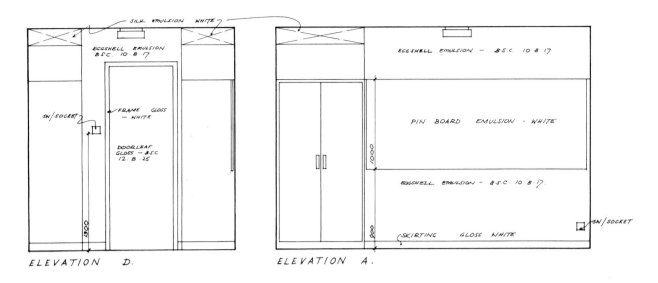

ELEVATION D.   ELEVATION A.

2.6 *(continued)*

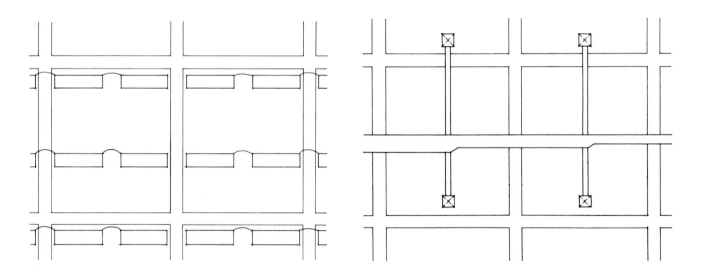

2.7 *Electrical layout at ceiling level*

2.8 *Air conditioning layout in ceiling void*

sense a general arrangement drawing and a finishes drawing and it will be coded G(45). It completes the sixth side of the cube for every room on that particular floor level.

This principle holds good whether the information is conveyed by CAD or manually.

Figures **2.7**, **2.8** and **2.9** show how the various disciplines concerned have dealt with their respective layouts for a particular area and how the G(45) ceiling finishes drawing (**2.10**) serves as a picture of the finished product, as well as providing a useful vehicle for information about applied finishes which it would have been difficult to provide in any other way.

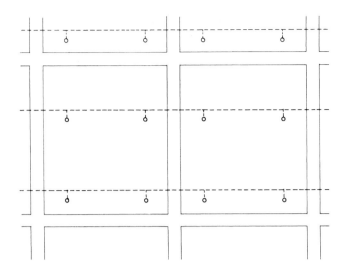

2.9 *Sprinkler layout at ceiling level*

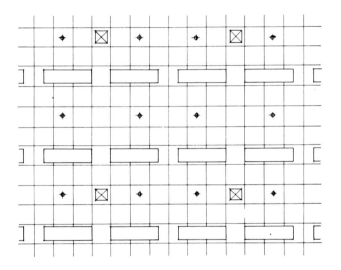

2.10 *Architect's general arrangement drawing of the ceiling finishes provides coordinating layout for everyone involved*

It should be noted here how much easier this correlation becomes with the use of CAD, where all the facets of information shown may be simply combined into one drawing file, as well as existing in their own right.

Roof plans

Roofs—particularly if they are flat roofs—are essentially just another floor and it might be thought pedantic to introduce separate codes for them. Admittedly quantity surveyors and others concerned with elemental cost analysis require the distinction, but drawing codes do not always help here. Is (**2.11**) a roof plan of the factory, for example, or is it a floor plan of the tank room?

It should be treated as a floor plan and coded accordingly as 'level number . . .'. This method of referring to all plans as 'levels' has the inbuilt (and on a very large project, the important) advantage that every plan level lies in a numerical sequence and that in consequence (if care is taken), general arrangement plans of any one level, no matter what their elemental subject, will possess the same number. The elementalised general arrangement plans of level 3, for example, would be numbered:

G(2-) 003
G(3-) 003
G(42) 003
G(43) 003
G(45) 003, etc.

On a large project this is of immense practical advantage to users of the drawing package because it offers them two ready sortations of the information. It is only necessary to assemble all the G(43) drawings, for example, to have the complete general arrangement information on floor finishes for the entire project. Assembling all general arrangement drawings whose sequential number is 003, on the other hand, provides every elementalised general arrangement plan for level 3.

It should be noted that in CAD, levels are effectively treated as horizontal sections. In fact, some automated CAD programs that generate plans, elevations and sections automatically from the 'model' can *only* work in this way.

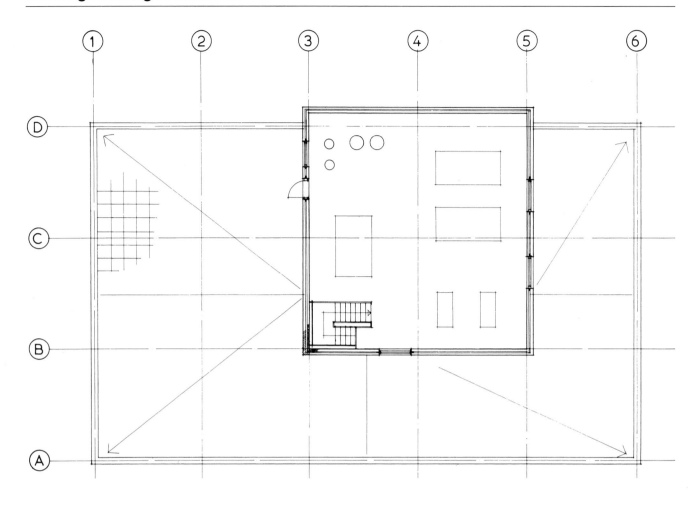

2.11 *Floor plan or roof plan? The problem is avoided if all plans are treated as 'levels'*

Some examples

It has been noted that even the most complex of projects is unlikely to engage more than a handful of the available elemental sub-divisions. By the same token, it would be a very simple project indeed that did not benefit from a degree of elementalisation. Two examples are given here:

- Project A—a multi-storeyed building of some two million pounds contract value (part of which has been used already in **2.1**, **2.2** and **2.3**, as well as **1.14**, **1.15** and **1.16** in Chapter 1).
- Project B—a small house.

General arrangement plans—primary elements

Note that CI/SfB Table 1 offers the following choice within the general summary code (2-):

(21)	Walls, external walls
(22)	Internal walls, partitions
(23)	Floors, galleries
(24)	Stairs, ramps
(27)	Roofs
(28)	Building frames, other primary elements.

In the larger of the two buildings—Project A—the decision was made to confine the architect's information about primary elements to a single (2-) drawing. A decision was made at about the same time in relation to the smaller and simpler Project B to sub-divide the primary elements to a greater degree. Since the reasons for arriving at these decisions were different in each case, they serve to illustrate the importance of thinking about what you are trying to achieve before actually starting to draw.

On Project A, which had a reinforced concrete frame and floor slabs, and which enjoyed the services of a structural consultant, it was deemed unnecessary, not to say inadvisable, for the architect's drawings to give constructional information about structural elements which were clearly the responsibility of the structural engineer. So floors (23), stairs (24), roofs (27) and frames (28), whilst appearing on the architect's primary element drawing (2-), nevertheless, remain in outline only. Against each of these elements appears a reference to the fact that the appropriate structural engineer's drawing should be consulted, thus satisfying the second of the two basic functions of a general arrangement plan—either to locate the element it deals with or to state where it may be found.

Of the other primary elements—and in this particular instance the walls and partitions are the primary consideration—the information given about them consists of statements as to where they are to be placed (i.e. dimensions from known reference points—sensibly, in this instance the structural grid); what they consist of (i.e. notes on their materials or reference back to more detailed specification information); and where further information about them may be found (i.e. coded references to relevant assembly details). The primary elements dealt with on this particular drawing, as distinct from primary elements dealt with on other general arrangement drawings, are identified by being emphasised in a heavier line than that used for the rest of the drawing.

The comparable (2-) drawing for the smaller of the two projects had obvious points of similarity but the reasoning behind its production was somewhat different. The building was of simple two-storeyed load-bearing brick construction, with simply supported timber roof and floor joists and timber staircase. There was no structural engineer, so the design and detailing of these structural elements devolved upon the architect.

Two primary elements drawings were therefore produced—a generic (--) drawing covering both external walls and internal partitions and a (27) drawing covering the roof construction. Both are shown in **2.12** and **2.13**.

It is worth making a point about the way in which the brickwork was described in each case because it illustrates the fundamentally common sense way in which all such decisions should be handled (**2.14**). In the larger building there were four different types of brickwork involved. These were:

1 A Class II engineering brick in cement mortar, used in manholes and certain works below ground.
2 A common brick to BS 3921 Part II, laid in a 1:1:6 mortar mix and used generally for all backings.
3 A sand–lime facing to BS 187, laid in 1:1:6 mortar to a Flemish bond and used generally as a facing brick to wall panels.
4 A hand-made fired clay facing brick, used in certain featured areas on the entrance facade and laid to a decorative pattern.

A schedule of brickwork types formed part of the specification, in which each type was fully identified and described. The reference Fg1/3 on the drawing would

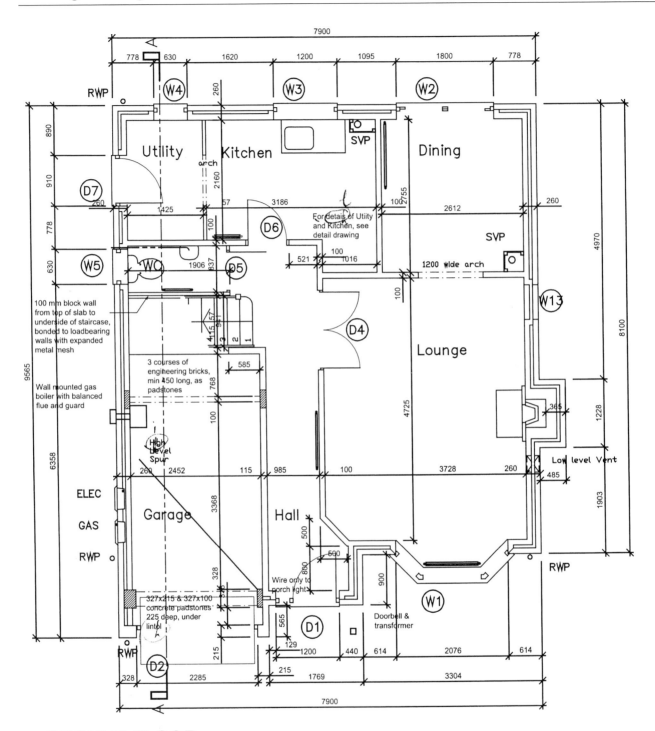

GROUND FLOOR

2.12 *Both primary and secondary elements are combined in this small building under the code (--) The Project in General. The simple nature of the building and the large scale of the drawing, made possible by its modest size, makes this feasible*

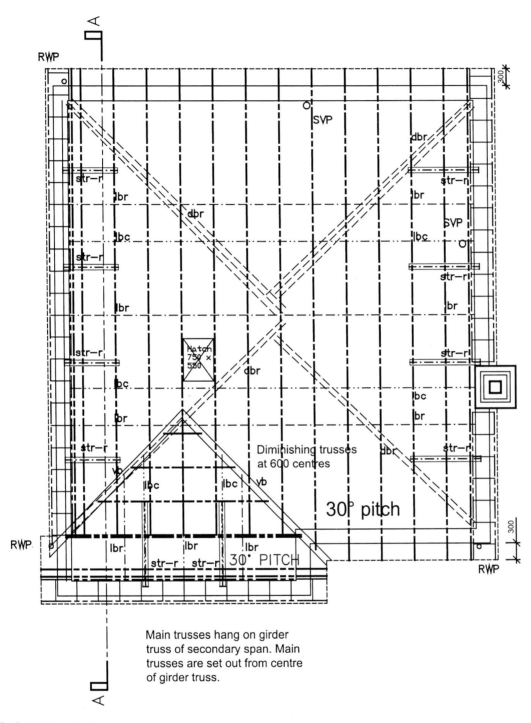

ROOF PLAN

2.13 *For clarity the roof construction layout is separated and coded (27)*

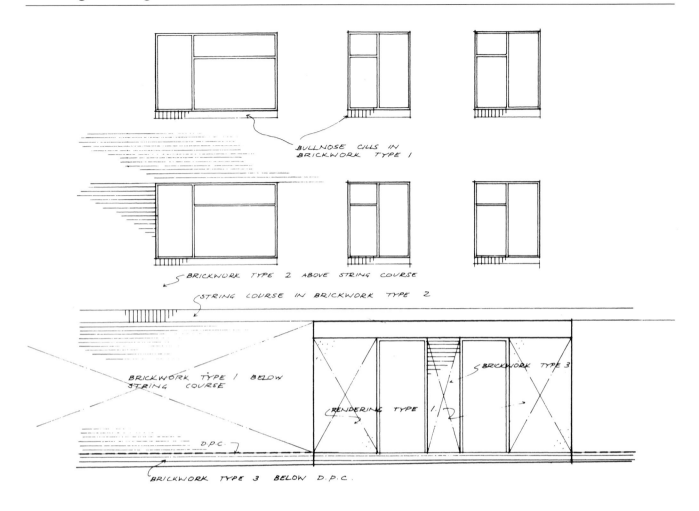

BULLNOSE CILLS IN
BRICKWORK TYPE 1

BRICKWORK TYPE 2 ABOVE STRING COURSE

STRING COURSE IN BRICKWORK TYPE 2

BRICKWORK TYPE 1 BELOW
STRING COURSE

BRICKWORK TYPE 3

RENDERING TYPE 1

D.P.C.

BRICKWORK TYPE 3 BELOW D.P.C.

2.14 *Elevations as a guide to external finishes not readily described in detail by other means*

indicate that it is the third type of brickwork in that schedule, which given that the project included the full CI/SfB nomenclature as part of its documentation would be found in the Fg (bricks and blocks) section of that specification. The intricacies of full CI/SfB coding is of course unnecessary unless so desired. 'Brickwork Type 3' would have been an equally specific identification, provided it were so described in the specification.

In the smaller project, however, only two types of brick were used—a common brick and a facing brick. So in this instance the description 'facing brick'—assuming the

specification has fulfilled its proper descriptive function—was perfectly adequate.

In neither case is it likely that the routine of the drawing office was disrupted a year later by someone telephoning from site to ask 'which brick goes here?'

Figure **2.15** shows the virtues of secondary structuring of drawings and the inherent flexibility of elementalisation when used with common sense and imagination. The project in question was one of a number dealing with a similar building type, each of which involved the appointment of a nominated sub-contractor for various

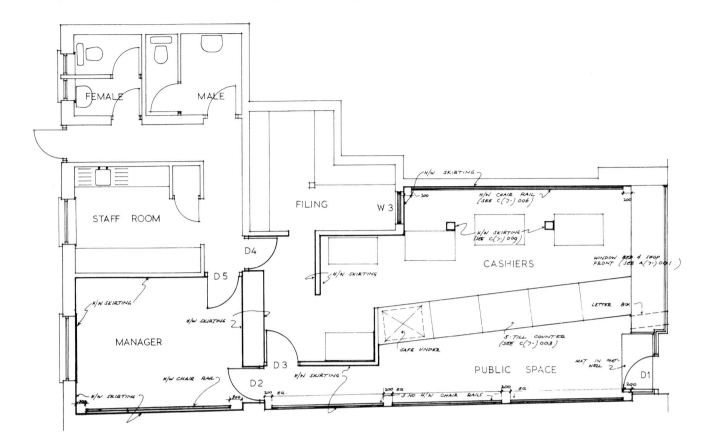

2.15 *Elementalisation used flexibly in practice. The general arrangement plan gives a clear exposition of the responsibilities of one sub-contractor—in this case the shopfitter*

shopfitting works. With certain elements—doors, pelmets and skirtings, for example—being carried out by the main contractor in some areas and by the shopfitter in others, it was important that the method of documentation employed should be capable of defining satisfactorily the limits of responsibility for each. It was also desirable that it should provide for separate packages of information being available upon which each could tender.

The method adopted in practice was to treat all the work of the shopfitter as a (7-) fittings element, regardless of rigid CI/SfB definitions and to record it on a (7-) general arrangement plan, while the work of the

main contractor appeared on separate general arrangement plans covering (2-) primary elements, (3-) secondary elements and (4-) finishes. Assembly drawings involving the work of both main contractor and shopfitter were referenced from all the relevant general arrangement plans and were included in both packages of information.

General arrangement plans—format

With very small buildings it is perhaps pedantic to ask that each of (two) plan levels be presented on a separate piece of paper when both fit happily one above the other on a single A2 sheet. In general, however, it is desirable that each sheet should be devoted to one plan

51

level only, the size of the building and the appropriate scale determining the basic size of sheet for the whole project.

Leave plenty of space on the sheet. Apart from the fact that this tends to get filled up with notes, etc. during the course of the drawing's production (the addition of three strings of dimensions on each face alone adds considerably to the original plan area of the drawing), it must be remembered that the drawing's various users will in all probability wish to add their own notes to the prints in their possession.

General arrangement elevations—external

Given the plan view and sufficient sections through an object, it is arguable that it is unnecessary to show it in elevation for the object to be fully comprehended. That so much often goes wrong on a building site, even with the benefit of elevations, is an illustration of the fact that the construction process often has little connection with formal logic; in practice, to erect a building without a set of elevations is like trying to assemble a jigsaw puzzle without the picture on the lid to refer to from time to time.

Nevertheless, it is as well to remember that the elevation's function is primarily informative rather than instructive, and that in consequence it should not be made to carry information more sensibly conveyed by other means.

If elevations are to be of relevance they must be complete and this means not just the four views—front, back and two sides—that sometimes suffice, but sectional elevations covering re-entrant points in the plan shape and the elevations of courtyards.

Remember too that the building consists of more than that which can be seen above ground. One of the more useful aspects of a properly produced set of elevations is that an indication can be given of the sub-structure

and of the building's relationship with the immediately surrounding terrain or pavings.

We have mentioned sectional elevations and we may as well deal here with general sections also, for in this context they serve the same purpose as the elevations, in that they present a general picture of the building without necessarily providing any specific information from which it can be built. They are of particular value to the contractor when he is planning the sequence of his operations on site, and for this reason those items of particular relevance to this function—the relationship of floor levels to one another and of the building to the ground are obvious instances—must be shown adequately.

Elevations too should carry grid lines and finished floor levels. Other than that they should be simply drawn, with all visible features included but not unduly elaborated.

Windows in particular tend to be overdrawn; there is really no point in elaborating glazing bars and beads when these aspects are going to be covered much more fully on the appropriate components drawings. Brick courses merely confuse the eye. We are not dealing here with an artistic pictorial simulation of the building but with a schematic factual representation.

There are four areas where elementalisation of the elevations should be considered, particularly on larger projects:

1   They may be used to locate external openings and this can be a helpful means of cross-reference back to the external openings schedule. All that is necessary is for the opening reference—(31)007, (31)029—to be given on the appropriate opening in the elevation. The practice, sometimes attempted, of using the elevation as the actual external openings schedule, is not to be recommended. More needs to be said about the average window than can sensibly be carried in a small box on a 1:100 elevation.

Such references are useful in relating a point on the elevation with its corresponding position on the plan, but the elevation should never be regarded as the primary source of reference for these components. Regardless of whether or not they appear on the elevations, it is essential that the references appear on the appropriate general arrangement plans. The references in **2.16** are to the external openings schedule.

2   They may be used to identify the type and extent of external finishes; this is a useful device, for it is not easy by any other means to indicate such things as patterned brickwork, the change from one type of bond or pointing to another, or soldier courses (see preceding **2.14**).

3   They may be used as both location drawings and schedule for cladding panels or ashlar facings (**2.17**).

4   They may be used to convey information about external plumbing and drainage services above ground level (**2.18**).

General arrangement sections

General arrangement plans in effect constitute a series of horizontal cross-sections through the building, spaced out so that one is taken at every floor level. This spacing is reasonable, since in practice the appearance of the horizontal section is most likely to differ from floor to floor and unlikely to differ between floor and ceiling.

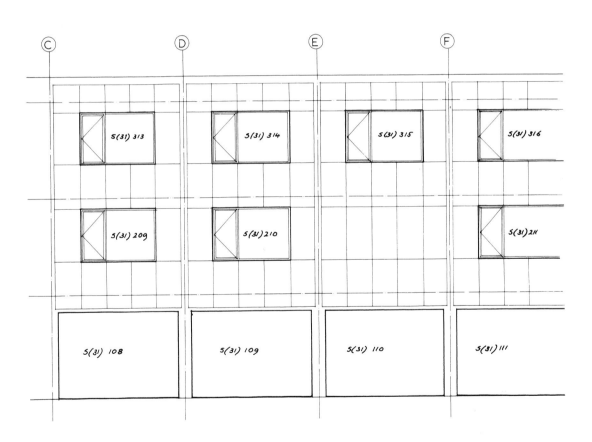

2.16   *Elevation as a secondary reference to window components. The reference S/31 leads back to the external seconday elements schedule, where the components are listed and classified*

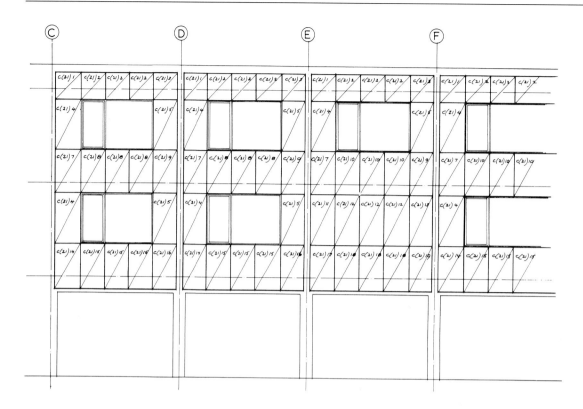

2.17 *With a limited range of panel types and with each panel's component drawing giving full information about it, the elevation itself forms an adequate schedule*

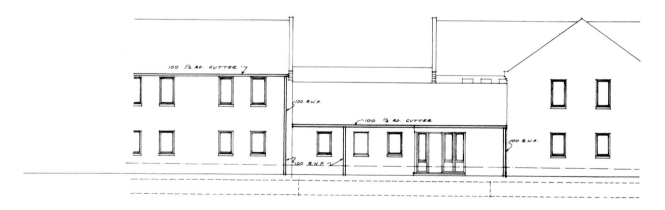

2.18 *Elevation giving information about external plumbing*

If a comparable series of vertical cuts were to be made through the building, again taking a fresh one whenever the appearance of the section changed, the result would be a very large number of sections indeed. Such vertical sections constitute a vital aspect of the information to be conveyed, yet their number must be limited to manageable proportions.

Fortunately, a large number of the possible sections tell us very little about the building. Figure **2.19** which

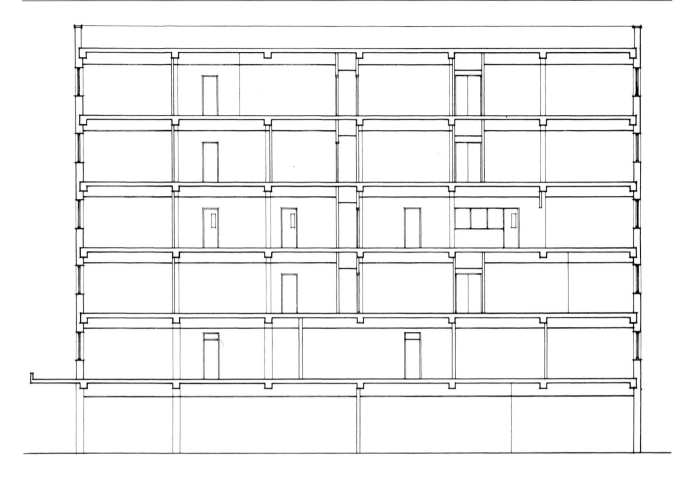

2.19 *Diagrammatic cross-section through a multi-storeyed building. Virtually all the information it gives may be conveyed more fully and intelligibly by other means. The frame will be built from the structural engineer's drawings; the doors will be manufactured from information to which the joiner is directed from the appropriate schedule; they will be installed in positions located on the floor plans; the construction of the external walls will be found on strip sections amplified as necessary by larger scale details. A section such as that shown has its functions but they are more likely to be advisory—i.e. letting the contractor see the sort of building he is embarking upon, rather than directly instructing him what to build and where to build it*

reduces the cross-section through a multi-storeyed building to a diagrammatic simplicity, will explain why.

Most of it is irrelevant to our understanding. The internal elevations of those rooms which are exposed by the section cut are not a very suitable medium for describing, for example, wall finishes, since the other three walls are not shown. It is true that we are shown the positions of doors in those walls but these are shown, and indeed dimensioned, much more comprehensively on the respective floor plans.

The heights of internal door frames may be derived whenever the section line passes through an internal wall coincident with a door opening, but the height of the frame may be obtained more readily from the

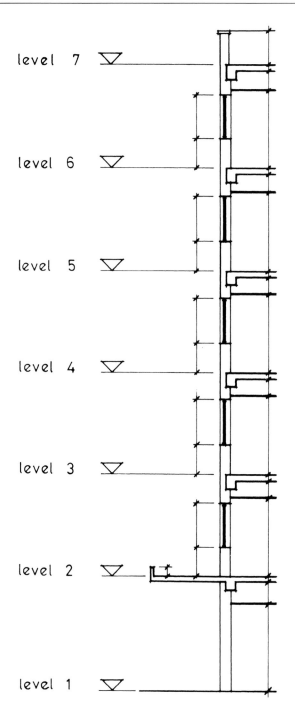

level 7

level 6

level 5

level 4

level 3

level 2

level 1

2.20 *Sectional cut confined to perimeter of the building*

component drawing of the doorset of which it will form part.

The only pieces of information it carries which are not readily obtainable from other sources in fact, are the height of the window sill, the height of the parapet, the relative floor levels and the thickness of the floor construction. Each of these items of information would be conveyed just as effectively if the section were confined to the narrow strip running through the external walls (**2.20**).

On a large project it is arguable that one such general section is useful to the contractor in describing generally the type of building upon which he is embarking. If provided, its purpose should be limited to this and the drawing regarded (and coded) solely as an information drawing.

Since the number of potentially different wall sections will be limited, the vast number of separate cross-sectional cuts through the building at first envisaged is reduced to manageable proportions. Such strip sections may also be used as a reference point for the detailed construction information which needs to be given about window head, window sill, parapet, footings and the junctions of floors with walls, and as such they may be regarded as forming part of the general arrangement information for the project.

There is little point in attempting to use the strip sections in themselves to convey this detailed information unless the building is so small, or so simple in its design, that a few such sections tell all that needs to be conveyed about the construction. In most instances the scale of the section and the number of times it will change around the building, will make it more sensible to treat the general arrangement section in almost diagrammatic terms.

Note that the floor levels are given and that the vertical dimensions (for example, to window sills) are given from

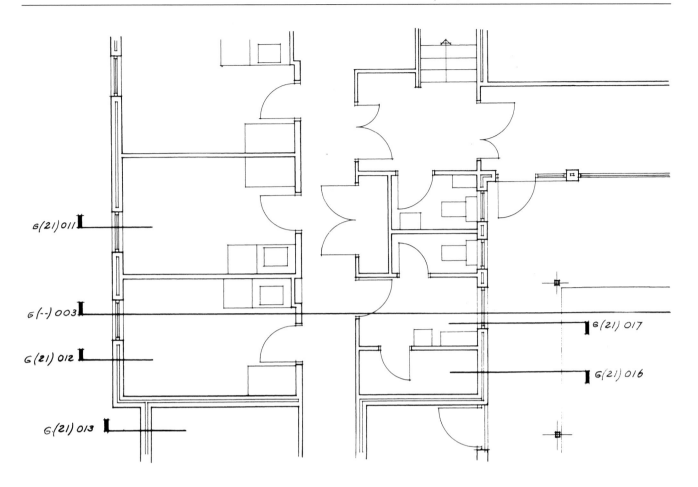

G(21) 011

G(--) 003

G(21) 012

G(21) 013

G(21) 017

G(21) 016

2.21 *General arrangement plans give references to general sections G(--) and strip section G(21). The former will be of the type shown in* **2.19**. *The latter will be similar in scope and function to* **2.20**

those floor levels to a datum which is readily achievable on site (for example, to the top of the last course of bricks), and to which the more comprehensive dimensioning contained in the subsequent assembly details may be referred.

There is no advantage in elementalising the general arrangement sections, although if CI/SfB coding is being used there is some logic in regarding them as G(2-) drawings, thus differentiating them from the G(--) general sections previously described and which fulfil a different purpose in the set.

The points around the building at which the strip sections are taken will, of course, be indicated on the general arrangement plans (**2.21**).

Site plans

The functions of the site plan are to show:

- The location of the building or buildings in relation to their surroundings.
- The topography of the site, with both existing and finished levels.

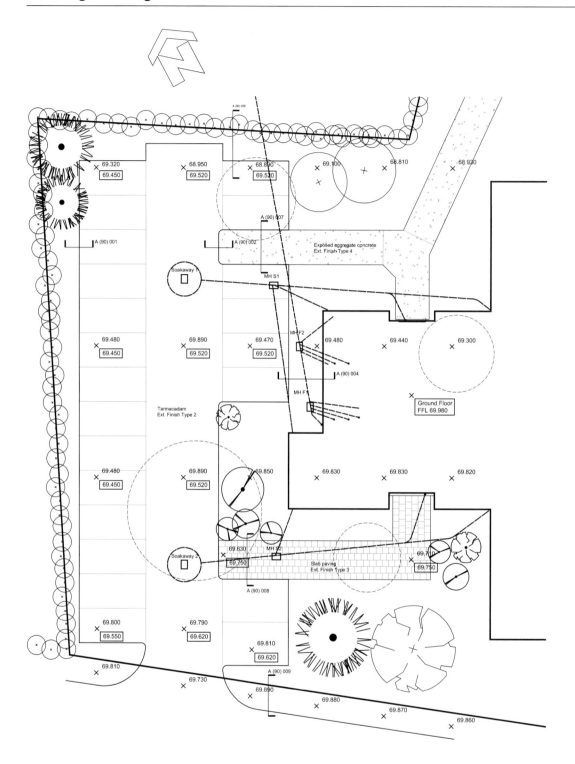

2.22 *A typical site plan. Information is given about new and existing levels as well as directions as to where other information may be found. (The information about levels is given here because the plan is to a sufficiently large scale and the small amount of earth moving makes it unlikely to form a separate contract—a good example of common sense prevailing over a more rigidly doctrinaire approach)*

- Buildings to be demolished or removed.
- The extent of earthworks, including cutting and filling, and the provision of banks and retaining walls.
- Roads, footpaths, hardstandings and paved areas.
- Planting.
- The layout of external service runs, including drainage, water, gas, electricity, telephone, etc.
- The layout of external lighting.
- Fencing, walls and gates.
- The location of miscellaneous external components—bollards, litter bins, etc. (**2.22**).

These are multifarious functions and some consideration has to be given to the desirability of elementalising them on to different drawings. The problem with site plans, however, is that these functions are closely interrelated. Incoming services may well share duct runs, which in turn will probably be related to the road or footpath systems; manhole covers will need to be related to paving layouts if an untidy and unplanned appearance is not to result.

There is a case for recording demolitions and earth movement on separate drawings. These are after all self-contained activities which will precede the other site works. Indeed, they may well form the subject of separate contracts and will often be carried out before other aspects of the site works have been finalised. Similarly, pavings are a finishing element which may

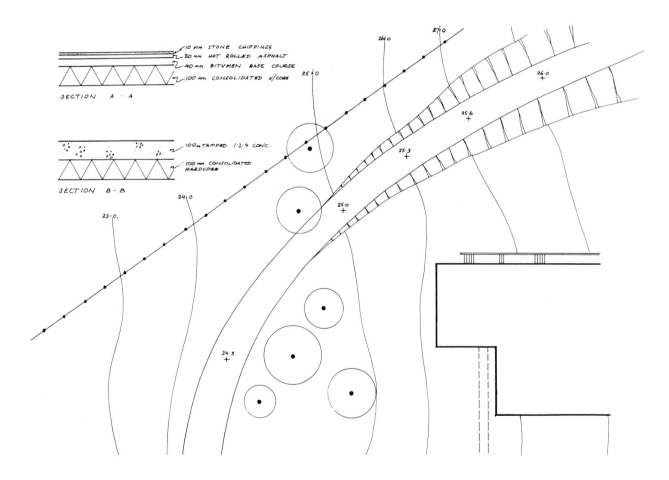

2.23 *Site plan with inset assembly details is not to be recommended. Such details form no part of what is essentially a general arrangement drawing*

benefit from separation into a drawing associated with service runs (and more particularly any manholes or inspection chambers within them).

When CAD is being used, of course, the problem is simplified into a question of layering the information. When the set is being drawn manually, however, the remaining site works are best recorded on a single drawing. If problems of clarity and legibility seem likely to arise by virtue of the work being unduly complicated, then common sense will dictate either further elementalisation or producing the drawing at an appropriately generous scale.

Most site plans that are unduly cluttered and difficult to read suffer from two faults:

1   They are at too small a scale for the information they are required to carry.
2   They attempt to include detailed information— large-scale sections of road construction are a frequent example—which apart from crowding the sheet would more logically appear separately among the assembly information of which they clearly form part.

Figure **2.23** is a good example of how not to do it. There is no room for the extraneous assembly information on what should be regarded solely as a general arrangement drawing, and it is interesting to speculate on the reasoning that led to its being there. In most cases it appears for one of two reasons. The first is that the detail was an afterthought, and since no provision had been made for its inclusion elsewhere in the set, it seemed providential that the site plan had this bit of space in one corner. The second arises in the belief that it helps the builder to have everything on the one sheet.

This latter misconception extends over a much wider field of building communications than the site plan and it cannot be refuted too strongly. No single document can ever be made to hold all the information necessary to define a single building element, let alone a single building. If to place the assembly section of the road on the same sheet as its plan layout was deemed to be helpful in this instance, then why not the specification of the asphalt and the dimensions of the concrete kerb as well? The road cannot be constructed, or indeed priced by the estimator, without them. The essential art in building documentation is not the pursuit of a demonstrably mythical complete and perfect drawing, but the provision of a logical search pattern which will enable the user to find and assemble all the relevant information rapidly and comprehensively.

Component, sub-component and assembly drawings

Component drawings

A component may be defined as any item used in a building which emanates from a single source of supply and which arrives on site as a complete and self-contained unit, whose incorporation into the building requires only its fixing to another component or components. Thus, a window is clearly a component, as is a manhole cover, a door, a section of pre-cast concrete coping, a mirror. So, for that matter, is a brick. (A brick wall would be an assembly.)

Two types of component should be distinguished:

1 There is the manufacturer's product, available off the builders' merchant's shelf, for which no descriptive drawing need be prepared. Such items as standard windows, sanitary fittings and proprietary kitchen units may be described uniquely by the quotation of a catalogue reference. If they are to be drawn at all then their draughting will be in the simplest terms, more for the avoidance of doubt in the minds of architect and contractor than for any other reason. Certainly any detail as to their method of construction will be at best redundant, and at worst highly amusing to the manufacturer.

2 There is the special item requiring fabrication—the non-standard timber window, the reception desk, the pre-cast concrete cladding panel—and in order that someone may make it as required, it is necessary for the architect to define quite precisely what it is he wants and (in many instances) how he wants it to be made.

Clearly it is the latter category that is of most concern at the drawing stage.

In both categories, however, a basic principle holds good. The component should always be defined as the largest single recognisable unit within the supply of a particular manufacturer or tradesman. An example will make this clear.

Figure **3.1** shows an elevation of a row of fixed and opening lights, contained within a pre-cast concrete frame and separated from each other by either a brick panel or a pressed metal mullion. How many window components are there? We may look at this in various ways, and all of them would have some logical force behind them. We could say, for example, that there were six window components, of which four were of type A and two were of type B (**3.2**). There is an attractive simplicity about this view.

It could be argued with equal justification, that we had in fact a single component, consisting of an assemblage of fixed lights, opening lights, coupling mullions and brick infill panels. The component, in fact, is everything held within the overall pre-cast concrete frame (**3.3**). This approach too has its attractions.

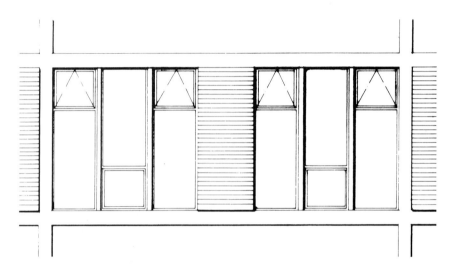

3.1   *How many window components in this assembly?*

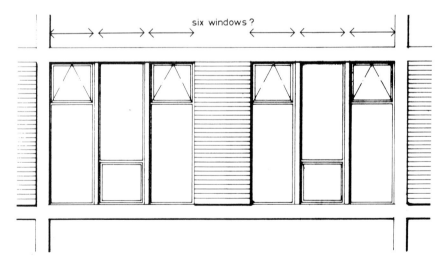

3.2   *Six window components?*

The correct procedure, however, will be to regard the whole assembly as consisting of two window components (**3.4**).

The key determining factor here is the supply of the component. It is reasonable to make the window manufacturer responsible for supplying the pressed metal mullions, but not for supplying the brick panel—and if he is to provide the coupling mullions, then it is rash and unnecessarily intrusive for the architect (inexperienced in this field) to take responsibility for the assembly junction between light and mullion. One of the problems associated with an increasingly factory-oriented building technology is ensuring a satisfactory fit when two components of different manufacture come together on site. Treating the component as embracing the coupling mullions at least puts one aspect of the problem squarely on the shoulders of the manufacturer, who is best equipped to deal with it.

This principle may be extended with advantage. If doors and frames are treated as two separate components the responsibility becomes that of the architect to ensure that the door meets the frame with the correct tolerances. If, however, the component is regarded as the complete doorset, then dimensional considerations apply only to the overall size of the frame and it is the joiner who ensures that door and frame fit one another. This is not passing the buck. Rather, it is putting

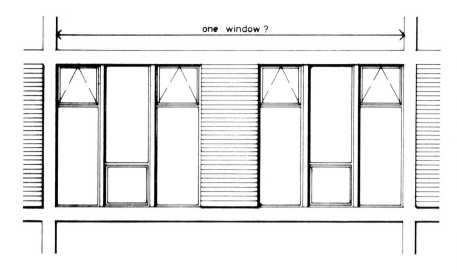

3.3 *One window component?*

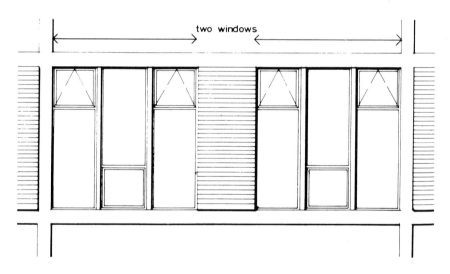

3.4 *This assembly is most sensibly regarded as having two window components*

back in the right hands a buck which the architect should never have picked up in the first place.

It is, of course, part of the architect's professional responsibility to ensure that he does not specify overall doorset sizes complete with frame dimensions which involve expensive non-standard doorleaf sizes. Similarly,

he must have the basic technical knowledge of joinery to ensure that he does not ask for a frame size which involves a third of the timber ending up as shavings on the joinery shop floor simply because the finished section was just too large to allow it to be run from a more economically sized sawn baulk.

Refinements in documentation method may simplify the process of building communications, but they cannot serve as substitutes for fundamental technical knowledge. (See also the notes on coordinating dimensions and work sizes in Chapter 4.)

Component drawings lend themselves to reuse within the office more than do other categories of drawing. One of the advantages of a comprehensive communications system is the facility it offers of standardising the format of such details, and hence enabling them to be used direct from one project to another. The resultant benefits in economy and consistency are obvious (**3.5**). For this reason a standard format should be considered and the drawing size will probably be smaller than that used for the rest of the project. (However, see the comments on this in Chapter 4.)

CAD of course lends itself well to this technique of storing details for reuse, the relevant details being held on disk until required. The ease with which details may be amended means that

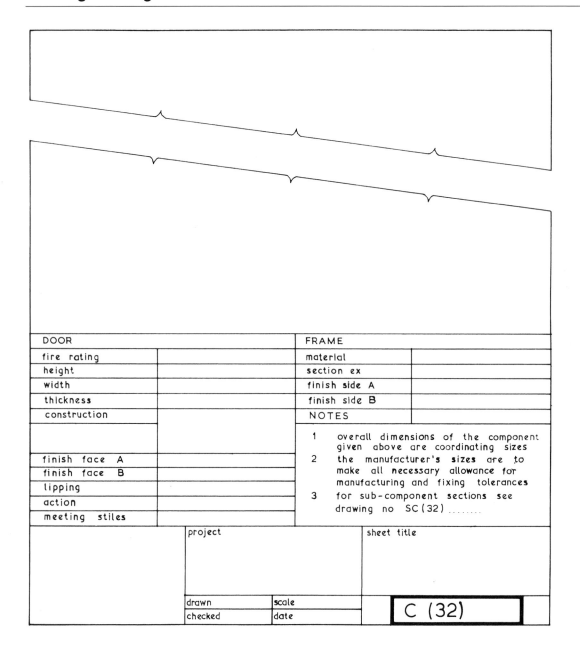

DOOR			FRAME		
fire rating			material		
height			section ex		
width			finish side A		
thickness			finish side B		
construction			NOTES		
			1 overall dimensions of the component given above are coordinating sizes		
finish face A			2 the manufacturer's sizes are to make all necessary allowance for manufacturing and fixing tolerances		
finish face B					
lipping			3 for sub-component sections see drawing no SC(32)		
action					
meeting stiles					

	project	sheet title	
	drawn / scale		
	checked / date	**C (32)**	

3.5 *Useful format for a door component drawing*

assembly drawings as well can benefit from this technique.

Figures **3.6**, **3.7** and **3.8** show three typical examples of component drawing. It should be noted that the general rule whereby drawing and specification information are segregated may be relaxed with advantage in the case of components, particularly when (for example **3.8**), they form part of a standard office library.

Note also that in **3.7** the term 'component' has been extended to embrace the method of fixing as well as the

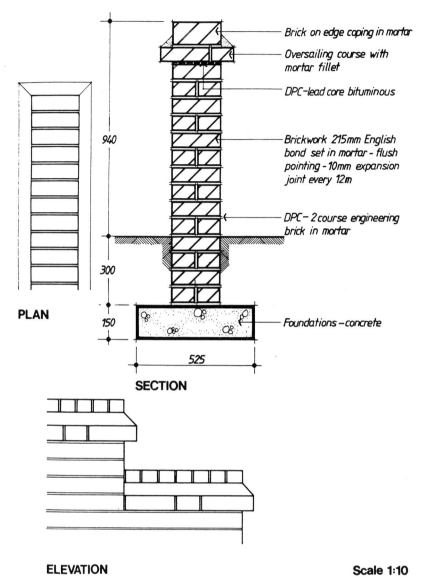

PLAN

Brick on edge coping in mortar

Oversailing course with mortar fillet

DPC-lead core bituminous

Brickwork 215mm English bond set in mortar - flush pointing - 10mm expansion joint every 12m

DPC- 2 course engineering brick in mortar

Foundations - concrete

SECTION

ELEVATION   **Scale 1:10**

3.6 *External works components such as this lend themselves to standardisation. Illustration from* Landscape Detailing *by Michael Littlewood, Architectural Press, London, 1984*

description of what is to be fixed. It is only common sense to treat such drawings as components rather than assemblies. Furthermore, the alternative fixing methods shown and the references back to the general arrangement drawing for overall sizes, make this one small detail of universal applicability when shelving of

this nature is required throughout even the largest project.

Sub-component drawings

These have a limited use and often the information they convey will be better shown on the component drawing. There are instances, however—particularly when a range of components is being dealt with of which the sizes and appearance differ but the basic construction remains constant—when it may be more economical to present details of the construction on a separate drawing.

For example, **3.9** shows two doorsets of different sizes and types. The basic sections from which they are fabricated are similar however and that fact has been acknowledged in this instance by the production of a sub-component drawing **3.10** to which the various components drawings refer.

The method is really best suited to large projects, or to those offices which have produced their own standard ranges of component details.

The assembly drawing

The juxtaposition of two or more components constitutes an assembly, and depending on the complexity of the arrangement and on how far it may be thought to be self-evident from other information contained elsewhere in the set, it will need to be drawn at an appropriate

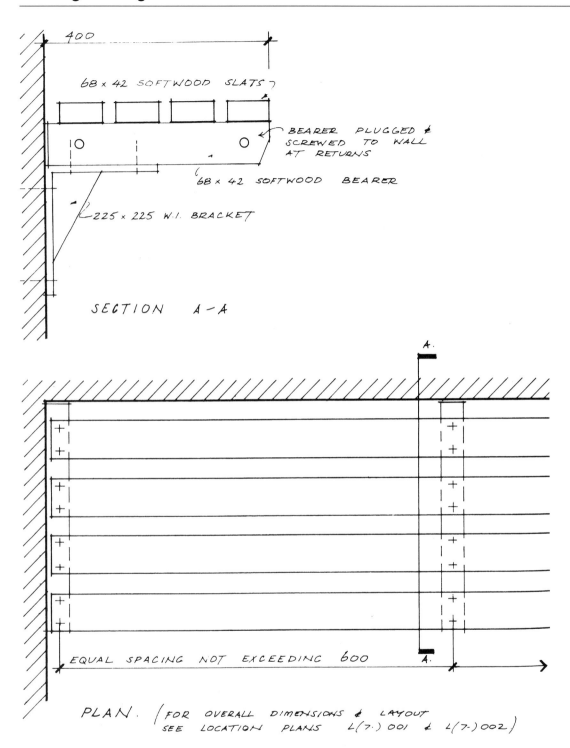

400

68 × 42 SOFTWOOD SLATS

BEARER PLUGGED &
SCREWED TO WALL
AT RETURNS

68 × 42 SOFTWOOD BEARER

225 × 225 W.I. BRACKET

SECTION   A–A

A.

EQUAL SPACING NOT EXCEEDING 600

A.

PLAN. (FOR OVERALL DIMENSIONS & LAYOUT
SEE LOCATION PLANS L(7·) 001 & L(7·) 002)

3.7 *Shelving treated as a component rather than as an assembly. An example of common sense overriding too rigid theories of classification*

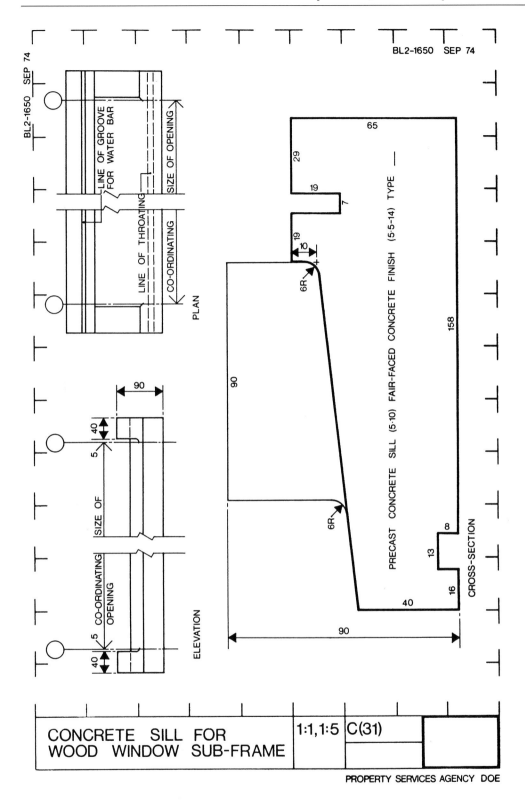

BL2-1650   SEP 74

BL2-1650   SEP 74

LINE OF GROOVE FOR WATER BAR

SIZE OF OPENING

LINE OF THROATING

CO-ORDINATING

PLAN

65

29

19

7

19

10

6R

PRECAST CONCRETE SILL (5·10) FAIR-FACED CONCRETE FINISH (5·5·14) TYPE

158

90

90

6R

8

13

16

40

CROSS-SECTION

90

40

5

SIZE OF

40

5

CO-ORDINATING OPENING

ELEVATION

CONCRETE SILL FOR WOOD WINDOW SUB-FRAME	1:1,1:5	C(31)	

PROPERTY SERVICES AGENCY DOE

3.8   *Component detail of concrete sill*

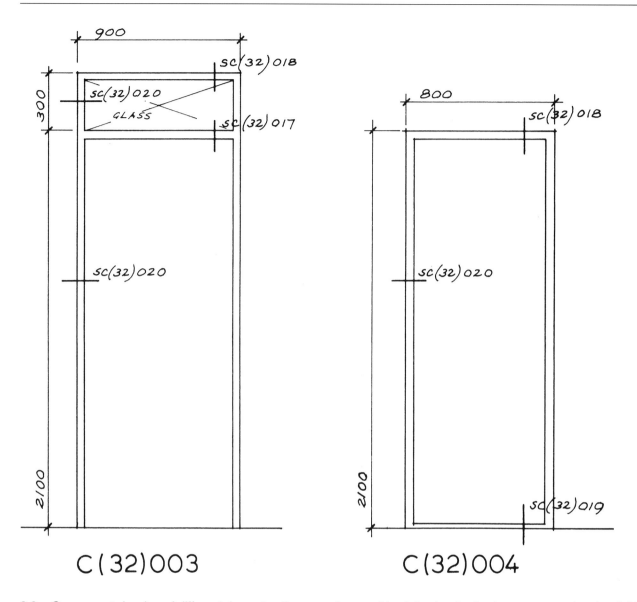

C(32)003   C(32)004

3.9 *Component drawing of different doorsets all cross-referenced back to standard sub-component drawing* **3.10**

scale for the benefit of the assembler. Figure **3.11**, taken from the UK Department of the Environment's PSA Library of Standard Details, is an assembly drawing. Figure **3.12**, part of Foster Associates' highly sophisticated detailing for the Willis, Faber and Dumas head office building in Ipswich, is another. A world of technology lies between them, but each drawing has in common that it defines how a number of component parts are to be put together.

With the assembly drawing we come to the very heart of the information package. If the general arrangement drawing is in many ways simply an ordered confirmation of planning decisions made long before, and the components drawing is frequently a documentation of the architect's judicious selection, the assembly drawing poses that most searching of all our questions, '*How* is it going to be built?' Before attempting to document his answer in a manner which is going to be acceptable to

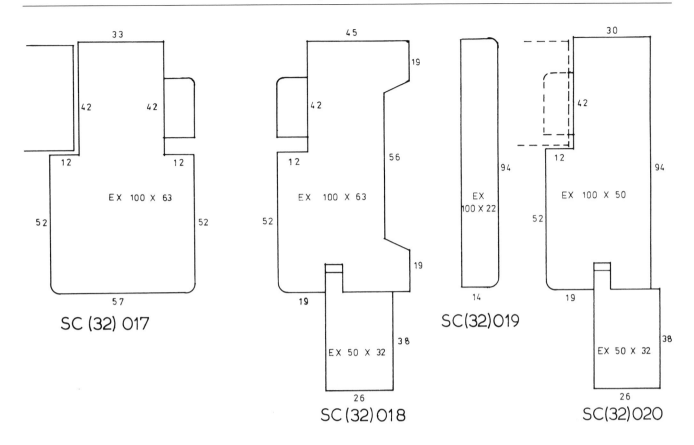

3.10 *Sub-component drawing illustrating details of the component itself. (Original scale full size)*

the users of the document, the detailer must not only be confident that he knows the answer but also be aware of the full implications of the question.

It was stated at the outset that this book is not intended as a textbook on building construction but it would be futile to pretend that the preparation of a set of working drawings can be regarded as an academic exercise, to be undertaken without reference to its content. Clearly, form and content interact, and the point is raised now because it is precisely here, in the area of assembly detailing, that the really fundamental questions of adequacy emerge:

• Will the construction function adequately?
• Is the method of presentation adequate?

• Does the range of detailing anticipate adequately all the constructional problems that will be encountered by someone trying to erect the building?

Check lists are of limited value. There is really no substitute for the complete involvement of the detailer in his task, for an intelligent anticipation of the possible difficulties, and for an alert awareness of the total problem while individual aspects of it are being dealt with. Nevertheless, it is useful at times to review one's work formally, if only because to do so concentrates the mind wonderfully. Since two distinct aspects of detailing are involved, two lists may be formulated.

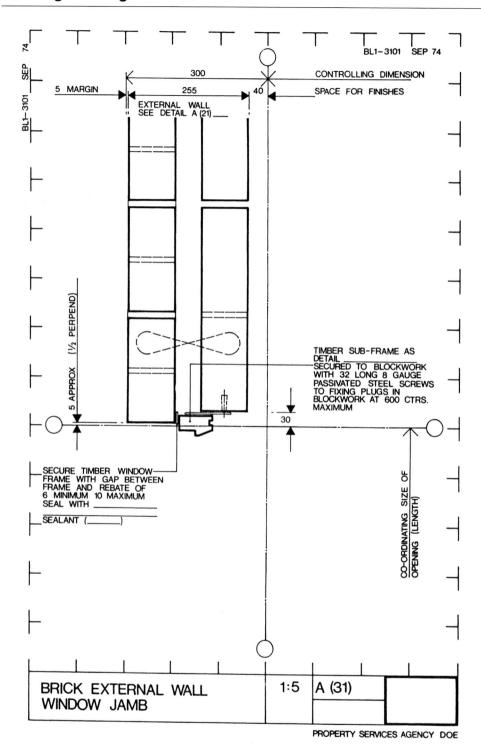

3.11 *Assembly detail taken from PSA Standard Library. Its simplicity contrasts sharply with the complexity of the detail illustrated in 3.12. What they have in common is that each conveys clearly and precisely the information needed by the operative carrying out the operation*

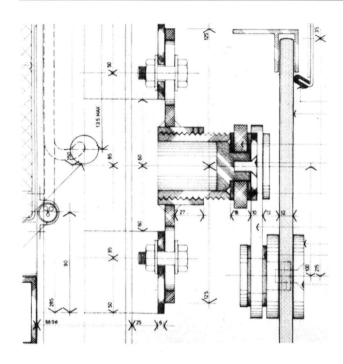

3.12 *Assembly detail from Willis Faber and Dumas Head Office Building. (Architects Foster Associates)*

The first, aimed at establishing the adequacy of the individual assembly detail, is a series of questions:

1   Is the chosen method of construction sound, particularly with regard to:
    • possible movement
    • water or damp penetration
    • condensation
    • cold bridging.
2   Has it been adequately researched, particularly if non-traditional methods or the use of proprietary products, are involved?
3   Is it reasonable to ask someone to construct it? Figure **3.13**—taken from a real but anonymous detail and calling for an improbably dexterous plasterer—is an example of the sort of thing that can occur when this question isn't asked.
4   What happens to the construction in plan (if the detail happens to be a sectional view) or in section (if the

detail happens to show a plan view?)
5   Is the result going to be acceptable visually, both inside and outside?
6   Does the information concerned give rise to any possible ambiguity or conflict with other information given elsewhere?

These questions are self-evident and the conscientious detailer should have them constantly in mind from the outset of the detailing. They are noted here because it is probably better to pose them once more, formally, on completion of the series of details, than to have to worry about them at random in the small hours of the morning at some later date.

The second check list, aimed at determining the completeness of assembly detailing throughout the building, is more capable of precise definition. The objective is to cover the building comprehensively, identifying those aspects which merit the provision of assembly information about them. A logical progression is essential and a suitable vehicle is readily to hand in CI/SfB Table 1 (see Chapter 1), for not only does this provide an analysis of the building in elemental form but it also affords a framework within which the necessary details, once they are identified, may be presented.

It should be noted here that almost all the assembly detailing with which the architect will be concerned is confined to the primary and secondary elements, sections (2-) and (3-) of CI/SfB Table 1. (The range of built-up fittings inherent in section (7-) should in general be regarded as components rather than assemblies.) Nevertheless, the exercise should be undertaken comprehensively.

The important things to note about assembly drawings are these:

1   *The scale must be appropriate to the complexity of the construction being detailed.* In practice this will

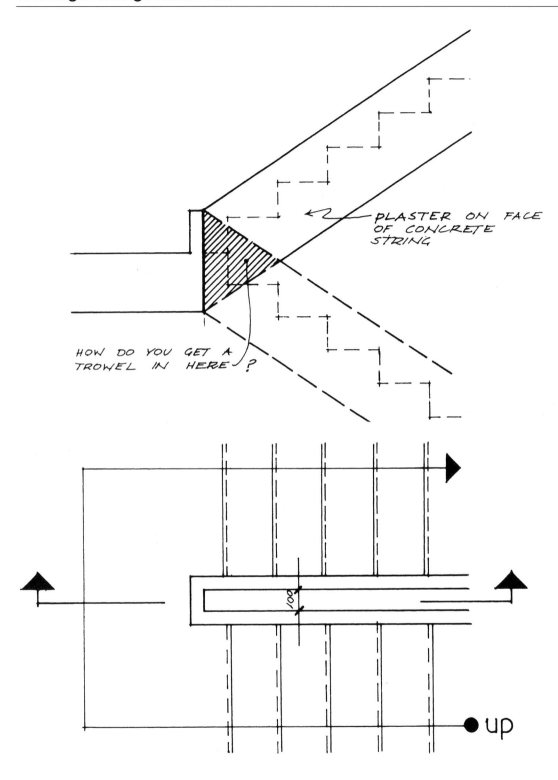

PLASTER ON FACE
OF CONCRETE
STRING

HOW DO YOU GET A
TROWEL IN HERE ?

up

3.13 *Not an easy task for any plasterer*

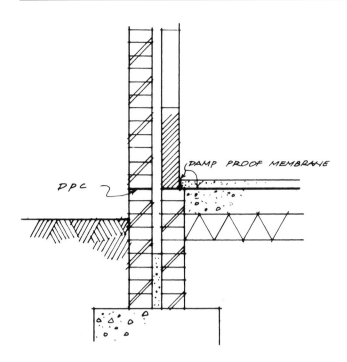

3.14 *Relatively simple detailing adequately conveyed at a scale of 1:20*

involve a scale of 1:20 being used for a wide variety of constructions, with a scale of 1:5 being used where greater detailed explanation is required—e.g. where the exact positioning of relatively small components such as bricks or tiles is a vital part of the information to be conveyed.

The level of draughting ability may well be a deciding factor when details are drawn manually. But don't be over-optimistic, the mere fact of drawing to a larger scale will force you into consideration of problems which might have been glossed over at a smaller scale. It is the operative ultimately who will be asking the questions and requiring the drawn answer. And he will be building full size. (In CAD, of course, the drawing files are created full size, and the ultimate scale is only applied when printing.)

Figures **3.14** and **3.15** at scales of 1:20 and 1:5, respectively, are appropriate examples of the information

it is necessary to convey. Note that the damp course in **3.14**, being a simple layer of lead-cored bituminous felt, can be shown adequately at the smaller scale, whereas the damp course in **3.15** is a much more complex piece of work, with all sorts of hazards should it be installed incorrectly and so justifies its more expansive 1:5 treatment. With CAD of course, where the details will generally be created full size, the same degree of detail will exist on the drawing file, to be reproduced at any scale deemed appropriate.

2   *The information given should be limited.* Perhaps concentrated is the better word. For it is more helpful to produce twenty assembly sections, each covering limited portions of the structure, than to attempt an elaborate constructional cross-section through the entire building purporting to give detailed information about almost everything.

Figure **3.16**, reduced here from its original scale of 1:20, is a good example of how not to do it. All that has been achieved is a very large sheet of paper, consisting of an internal elevation at an inappropriately large scale surrounded by a margin of detailing which through necessity has been portrayed at a smaller scale than would have been desirable. The drawing has clearly taken a considerable time to produce. This in itself may well have led to some frustration on the part of the builder or the quantity surveyor, who needed urgently to know the damp course detailing in the bottom left-hand corner but had to wait for the gutter flashing at the top right-hand corner to be finalised before the drawing could be issued to him.

At the end of the day we have been shown in some detail what happens to the construction along a more or less arbitrary knife cut through the building at one point. It is to be hoped that the detailing is consistent right round the perimeter, because the manual detailer is not going to be anxious to repeat the exercise whenever the construction changes. Were he to do so he would find

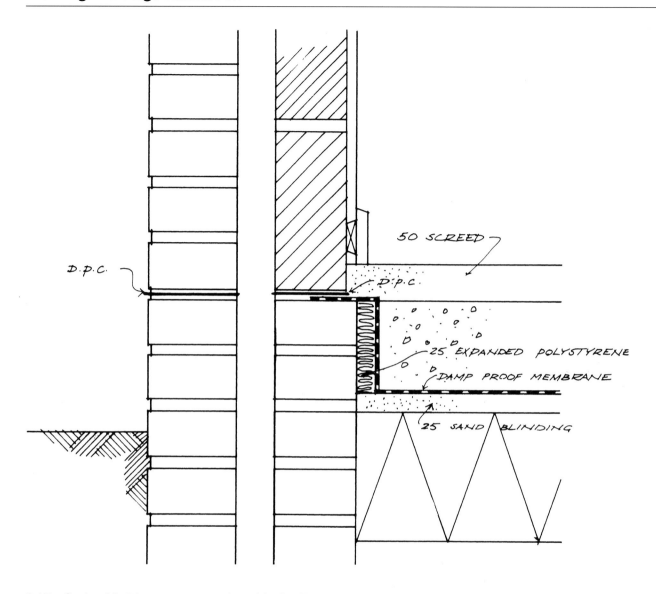

3.15 *Scale of 1:5 is necessary to show this detailing adequately*

himself redrawing 80 per cent of the information time and again in order that changes in the other 20 per cent could be properly recorded. The use of CAD makes this process a lot easier and more rapid but it is still a somewhat pointless exercise.

The more sensible way to deal with providing this sort of information is to prepare the assembly details in conjunction with, and related back to, the series of sections described and advocated in the previous

section on general arrangement drawings. The relevant information would then be cross-referenced on the lines of **3.17** and **3.18**.

3   *The assembly drawing should not be used to convey unnecessarily detailed information about the components from which it is to be produced.* Consider the assembly section shown in **3.19**. The window frame is a standard section and will be bought in from a supplier ready for fixing into the structural opening. There was no need

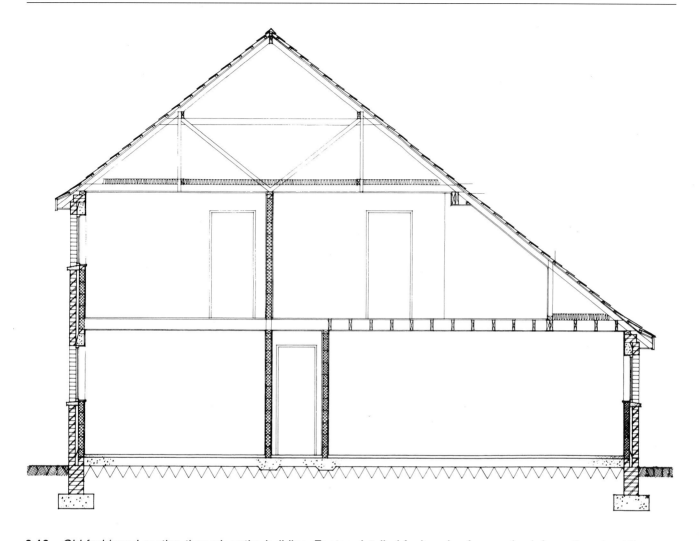

3.16 *Old-fashioned section through entire building. Far too detailed for its role of conveying information about the form and nature of the building; insufficient for anyone to build from it with confidence*

therefore to detail so lovingly and so explicitly the profiles of the frame and sub-frame, right down to the glazing beads and the throatings—they are matters of moment to the manufacturer in his workshop, not the erector on site. (The matter of prime importance to the erector, the method of fixing, is not mentioned at all—let us charitably assume that the point had been covered in the specification.) The only piece of information this assembly detail need convey about the window is its relationship to the surrounding components.

The detail might have been produced more simply and speedily as shown in **3.20**.

4   *The information conveyed should be both comprehensive and, within the limits already defined for an assembly drawing, exhaustive.* It should be comprehensive in the sense that the individual detail must contain all that the operative is going to need when he comes to that point on site. The detail may have been produced primarily to show the detailing of the window

75

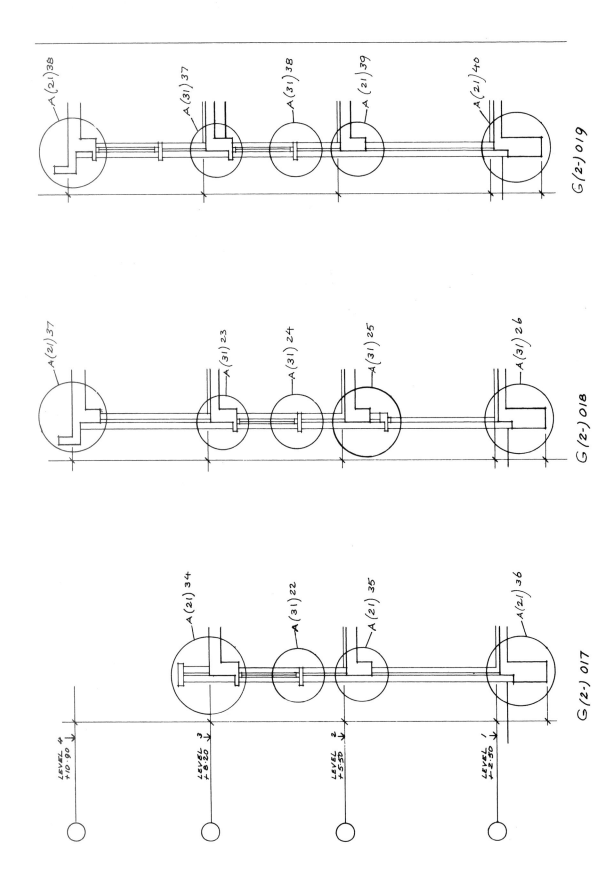

3.17 *General arrangement sections provide references to where more detailed assembly information may be found*

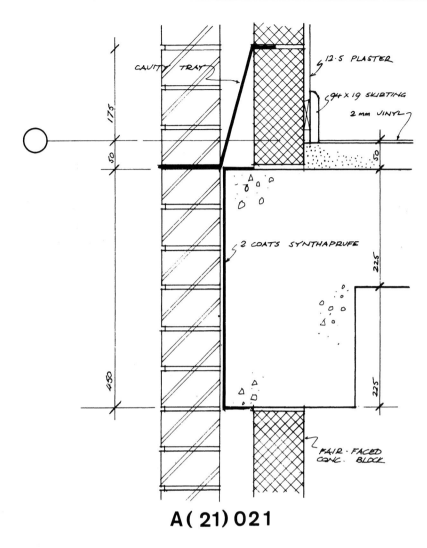

CAVITY TRAY

175

50

12·5 PLASTER

94 X 19 SKIRTING

2 mm VINYL

50

2 COATS SYNTHAPRUFE

225

225

450

FAIR·FACED
CONC. BLOCK

A (21) 021

3.18 *Assembly sections derived from* **3.17**

sill at a particular junction but if it purports to show this junction then others will expect to use it for their own purposes and it is no use being explicit about the window sill and vague about the wall finish beneath it. An assembly drawing is, by definition, a correlation of *all* the elements and trades involved.

So too the information should be exhaustive in the sense that no aspect of the construction, no variant on a basic detail, should be ambiguous or left to the discretion of the operative. 'Typical details' are just not good enough.

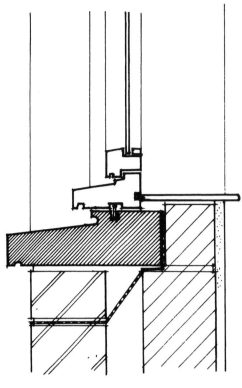

3.19 *Unnecessary elaboration wastes time and helps nobody*

Coding assembly drawings

A complete system for coding the drawing package is discussed in Chapter 5 but a note here on the coding of the drawings illustrated in **3.17**, **3.18** and **3.20** may be helpful.

The general arrangement sections (**3.17**) are coded G for general arrangement; (2-) for primary elements (see notes on general arrangement sections earlier for the reasoning on this); and 017, 018 and 019 because that is their sequence in that particular series.

The references in the circles are to external wall details or to external wall opening

It is not unreasonable to give a (21) coding to the section shown in **3.18**, for it clarifies the construction of an external wall. But then so does the section illustrated in **3.20**. Why not code that (21) also?

The answer is that it would be perfectly in order to do so and if you elected to produce a series of details devoted to the assembly problems encountered in constructing the external walls, then you would code A(21)001, etc. accordingly. But it is more likely that in commencing a series of details showing the *junctions* of two elements—for example, the junction of external openings with the external walls within which they sit—you would find it more convenient, and a better guarantee that you had covered the subject comprehensively, to produce a series of external openings assembly details—and these would naturally fall into the A(31) series.

The examples of assembly details illustrated have consisted of vertical sections through a particular construction but of course the plan section also requires illustration and enlargement at certain key points—door and window jambs, for example.

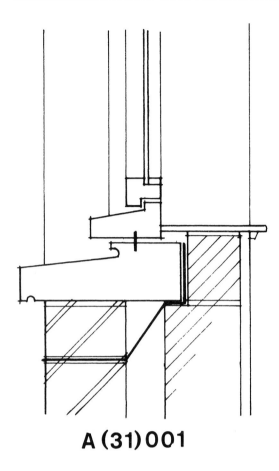

A (31) 001

3.20 *Simplified version of 3.19 gives adequate information to all concerned*

details (i.e. to windows) and are therefore coded, respectively: A for assembly, (21) for external walls, followed by their number in the sequence of such details; and A for assembly, (31) for external openings, followed by their number in the sequence of such details.

The assembly section shown in **3.18** is coded: A for assembly; (21) for external walls; and 021 because that is its number in the series.

The assembly section shown in **3.20** is coded: A for assembly; (31) for external openings; and 001 because it is the first in that series.

Where this is the case and where space allows, it is better to group plans and sections together by their common element rather than to produce a series of plan details on one sheet and a series of section details on another. Everyone on site concerned with forming the window opening and with fixing the window into it, will then have the relevant information readily to hand.

The schedule

(See also the section on schedules in Chapter 1.)

There are two distinct types of schedule.

78

There is the straightforward list of items, complete in itself, which adds nothing to information which may be obtained elsewhere in the drawings or the specification. What it does is present this information in a more disciplined and readily retrievable form. A list of lighting fittings, collected on a room-by-room basis, is an example, providing a convenient document for the electrical contractor who has to order the fittings and a useful check list with which the architect can reassure himself that none has been overlooked.

Schedules of manholes, of sanitary fittings and of ironmongery are others of this type, as indeed is the drawing schedule.

Such schedules, carrying descriptive rather than graphical information, are better typed than drawn and their natural home is more likely to be within the covers of the specification or bills of quantities than the drawing set.

The other type of schedule is also component-oriented but in addition to being a list it provides an essential link in the search pattern information by giving pointers as to where other information is to be found. Such schedules are of the type envisaged in **1.9** and commented upon in Chapter 1. A useful format is shown in **3.21**.

Note that what is shown is neither a door schedule nor a window schedule but an 'openings schedule'. It is important to maintain this concept if the drawing set is being structured using CI/SfB, because CI/SfB acknowledges only 'openings in external walls', 'openings in internal walls', 'openings in floors' and 'openings in roofs'. All components filling such openings require to be treated as part of the opening and hence are scheduled accordingly.

Even if use is made of some other elemental form of coding, however, it is still of advantage to follow the same pattern, for it enables information to be included in the schedule both about openings which are filled by no component—an arched opening, for example, or an unsealed serving hatch—and about openings filled by components which are neither doors nor windows—ventilator grilles, for example.

A form of schedule best avoided is what might be termed the 'vocabulary schedule'. An example is shown in **3.22**. The basis of this type of schedule is the vertical tabulation of a list of components or rooms, and the horizontal tabulation of an exhaustive list of ancillaries. The disadvantages of this method are two-fold. It is not always easy to be exhaustive in assessing at the outset the range of possible ancillaries, with the result that the subsequent introduction of another item disrupts the tabulation. And the use of dots or crosses to indicate which ancillary is required is visually confusing and prone to error.

A more rational way of dealing with this ironmongery schedule would be to collect the individual items of ironmongery into a series of sets and to indicate which set is required against the individual door or window component in the openings schedule illustrated in **3.21**. The listing of ironmongery sets would then be as shown in **3.23**, and the addition to the schedule would appear as in the 'Ancillaries' column in **3.24**.

Pictorial views

The use of perspective sketches, axonometric and exploded views should not be overlooked as a means of conveying information which might be difficult to document in more conventional forms. (The ability of CAD to produce three-dimensional information is of obvious benefit here.) Nor should the value of pictorial elevations, perspectives, photo montages and models be discounted as an aid to the contractor. Photographs of existing buildings are invaluable to an estimator when

OPENING				COMPONENT		ASSEMBLY DRAWINGS REFERRING			
OPENING NO	ROOM NAME/NO	COORDINATING DIMS		TYPE/ DRG. NO	DESCRIPTION	JAMB (VIEWED FROM INSIDE ROOM)		HEAD	CILL
		HEIGHT	WIDTH			L.H.	R.H.		
(32)G001	G/2	2100	900	C(3-)001	DOOR	A(3-)002	A(3-)002	A(3-)002	—
(32)G002	G/1	2100	900	C(3-)001	"	A(3-)002	A(3-)002	A(3-)002	—
(32)G003	G/2	2100	900	C(3-)001	"	A(3-)002	A(3-)002	A(3-)002	—
(32)G004	G/6	2100	800	C(3-)002	"	A(3-)003	A(3-)003	A(3-)001	—
(32)G005	G/6	2100	800	C(3-)002	"	A(3-)001	A(3-)001	A(3-)001	—
(32)G006	G/7	2100	800	C(3-)002	"	A(3-)003	A(3-)003	A(3-)001	—
(32)G007	G/7	2100	800	C(3-)002	"	A(3-)001	A(3-)001	A(3-)001	—
(32)G008	G/5	AS MANUFACTURER'S CAT.		MAGNET MCF 26	"	—	—	—	—
(31)G009	G/4	"	"	MAGNET MCF 36	"	—	—	—	—
(32)G010	G/2	1100	300	C(38)002	VISION PANEL	A(38)002	A(38)002	A(38)002	A(38)002
(32)G011	G/1	SHOP FITTERS' SUPPLY		—	WICKET GATE	—	—	—	—

3.21 *Useful format for an openings schedule*

pricing demolition or rehabilitation work and a model, or a photograph of one, will often demonstrate site management problems to the contractor's planning team more succinctly than a collection of plans and sections.

CAD programs printing raster printers (inkjets and lasers) will allow photographs to be incorporated into the rest of the drawings. Such pictorial aids should be clearly defined as being for informational purposes only and not possessing any contractual significance.

Specification

The function of the specification in relation to a competent and comprehensive set of drawings may be defined quite simply. It is to set out quality standards for materials and workmanship in respect of building elements whose geometry, location and relationships to one another have been described by means of the drawings.

It follows therefore that in a properly structured information package neither specification nor drawings should trespass upon the other's territory. If the drawing calls for roofing felt then it need describe it simply as that—'roofing felt', or 'built-up felt roofing'. If only one type of built-up roofing felt construction is to be used on the project then that simple description suffices. If more than one, then 'built-up felt roofing type 1' will be a sufficient indication of intent. To the specification will then fall the task of describing in detail just what 'built-up roofing felt type 1' is to consist of.

Conversely, the specification is no place for instructions such as 'Cover the roof of the boiler house in three

Door No	1 pair of lever handles	2 back plate with ① L.H.	3 back plate with ① R.H.	4 pair of knobs 47 mm	5 back plate with ④ L.H.	6 back plate with ④ R.H.	7 Taylor's spindle	8 push plate 150 × 75	9 push plate 225 × 75	10 escutcheon (for locks)	11 escutcheon (for latch)	12 single pull handle 150	13 single pull handle 225 mm	14 door stop - floor	15 door stop - wall	16 indicator bolt	17 flush bolt - 225 mm	18 barrel bolt - 100 mm	19 mortise panic bolt	20 cylinder lock	21 overhead door closer	22 H.D. ditto	23 floor spring - single	24 floor spring - double	25 upright mortise lock for ①	26 upright mortise lock for ④	27 upright mortise latch	28 kicking plate - 150 mm	29 kicking plate - 225 mm
G/11								●				●											●						●
G/12								●				●											●						●
G/13	●	●								●		●		●													●		
G/14	●	●								●				●							●						●		
G/15	●		●							●				●													●		
G/16	●		●							●			●								●						●		
1/01			●		●	●			●								●									●			
1/02	●	●																									●		
1/03	●	●																									●		
1/04	●		●																								●		
1/05							●				●					●					●								
1/06	●		●																								●		
1/07	●		●																								●		
1/08							●				●					●					●								
1/09	●	●																									●		
1/10				●	●		●		●																●				
1/11	●	●							●									●							●				
1/12	●		●							●																	●		
1/13	●		●						●									●							●				

3.22 *'Vocabulary' type of schedule. It is dangerously easy to get a dot in the wrong place*

SET NO	ITEM	MAKE	CAT. REF.
1	pair of lever handles	Modric	A 3001
	pair of back plates	"	A 6001
	pair of insert escutcheons	"	A 2104
2	pair of knobs (47 mm)	"	A 2501
	pair of back plates	"	A 600
3	pair of lever handles	"	A 3001
	pair of back plates	"	A 6001
	pair of insert escutcheons	"	A 2104
	overhead door closer	"	A 9106
4	push plate	"	A 6800
	single pull handle	"	A 1202
	indicator bolt	"	A 5001
	overhead door closer	"	A 9106

3.23 *Lists of ironmongery collected into sets*

layers of built-up felt roofing.' If a specific roof surface is to be so covered, then it is the function of the drawings to tell everybody so, when the full extent of the covering and the possible operational problems in achieving it may be clearly and simply described.

This simple differentiation between the roles of drawings and specification will enable each to fulfil its true function properly.

Conversion, alteration and rehabilitation

It is now necessary to look at the methods described previously and to see how far they are applicable to the description of work to existing buildings.

To dispose of the simple matters first, straightforward extensions to buildings present no problem. They are in every respect new pieces of building and there is no

OPENING				COMPONENT		ASSEMBLY DRAWINGS REFERRING				ANCILLARIES		
OPENING NO	ROOM NAME/NO	COORDINATING DIMS		TYPE/ DRG. NO	DESCRIPTION	JAMB (VIEWED FROM INSIDE ROOM)		HEAD	CILL	LINTOL TYPE / DRG. NO.	IRON-MONGERY SET NO.	LOCK REF.
		HEIGHT	WIDTH			L. H.	R. H.					
(32) 001	G/2	2100	900	C(3-)001	DOOR	A(3-)002	A(3-)002	A(3-)002	—	TYPE A	3	A B304
(32) 002	G/1	2100	900	C(3-)001	''	A(3-)002	A(3-)002	A(3-)002	—	TYPE A	2	A B301
(32) 003	G/2	2100	900	C(3-)001	''	A(3-)002	A(3-)002	A(3-)002	—	TYPE B	2	A B301
(32) 004	G/6	2100	800	C(3-)002	''	A(3-)003	A(3-)003	A(3-)001	—	NONE	4	–
(32) 005	G/6	2100	800	C(3-)002	''	A(3-)001	A(3-)001	A(3-)001	—	NONE	4	–
(32) 006	G/7	2100	800	C(3-)002	''	A(3-)003	A(3-)003	A(3-)001	—	NONE	4	–
(32) 007	G/7	2100	800	C(3-)002	''	A(3-)001	A(3-)001	A(3-)001	—	NONE	4	–

3.24 *The openings schedule shown in **3.21** extended to give information about ironmongery sets*

reason why the methods adopted for any other new building and the conditions relating to their use should not apply.

Where information needs to be given about work to existing structures, two additional aspects need consideration which are not present in entirely new work. One is the question of demolitions, particularly demolitions within a structure. The other is the question of repairing and making good.

Whenever any demolition of existing structures is involved, no matter how modest, it is preferable to show it on a separate drawing—to regard it, in fact, as one more element in the elementalised set. The expression 'demolitions' is to be interpreted widely in this connection, including such items as forming an opening in an existing wall as well as more major demolitions involving entire sections of the building. The correct way to deal with an opening to be cut in an existing brick wall to take a new door and frame is shown in **3.25**. The

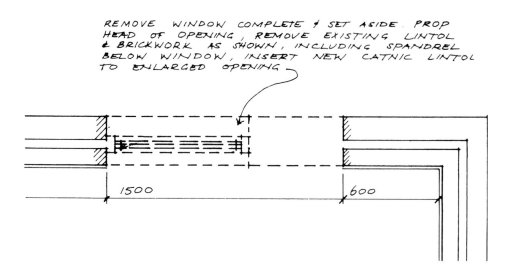

REMOVE WINDOW COMPLETE & SET ASIDE. PROP
HEAD OF OPENING, REMOVE EXISTING LINTOL
& BRICKWORK AS SHOWN, INCLUDING SPANDREL
BELOW WINDOW, INSERT NEW CATNIC LINTOL
TO ENLARGED OPENING

1500   600

3.25   *Demolition drawing covering formation of new opening in an existing wall*

drawing deals with the forming of the opening as a single activity, including the insertion of the new lintel over. It could hardly be dealt with otherwise by the builder. The drawing showing the new work **3.26** refers only to the new door and frame, inserted in what is by then an existing opening.

Note that it would be wrong for the drawing showing new works to make reference to the opening having been formed under the same contract. To do so would invite the possibility of the estimator including the item twice. Neither is the routine note 'make good to plaster and finishes' included on either drawing. Such a general instruction, which will presumably apply to a number of such door openings throughout the project, is more appropriate to the specification or schedule of works.

Generally speaking, a single demolition plan for each floor will suffice, but if there are complexities of a special nature to be covered then the mode of conveying the information may need to be more elaborate. Figure **3.27**, for example, shows the demolition drawing of a reflected ceiling plan, where the fact that certain suspended ceiling tiles and light fittings were to be removed is

carefully separated from the new work which is to replace them (**3.28**), as well as from the alterations to internal partitions, etc. which are covered on another sequence of drawings.

Simple items of making good, such as the replacement of areas of plaster, or the overhauling and repair of windows, are often most simply covered by scheduling on a room-to-room basis. If only two square metres of plaster are to be replaced in a given room, it is presumably obvious enough to all concerned which two square metres are referred to, without the necessity of precisely locating them on an internal elevation. Written description, in fact, is often better than graphical instruction in much rehabilitation work.

If CI/SfB coding is being adopted for the set then demolition drawings will normally be given a (—) 'project in general' code, leaving the more detailed code references for application to the new works.

One extremely important point is often overlooked in drawings of alteration work, with unfortunate consequent effects. It is absolutely vital that everyone should be clear

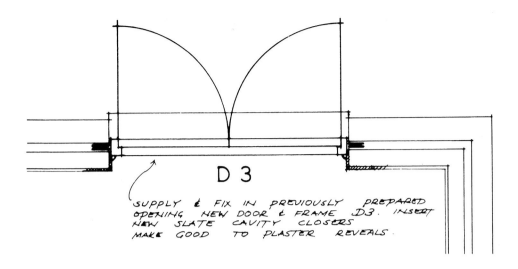

D 3

SUPPLY & FIX IN PREVIOUSLY PREPARED
OPENING NEW DOOR & FRAME D3. INSERT
NEW SLATE CAVITY CLOSERS
MAKE GOOD TO PLASTER REVEALS.

3.26 *Drawing covering installation of door and frame in the opening formed in* **3.25**

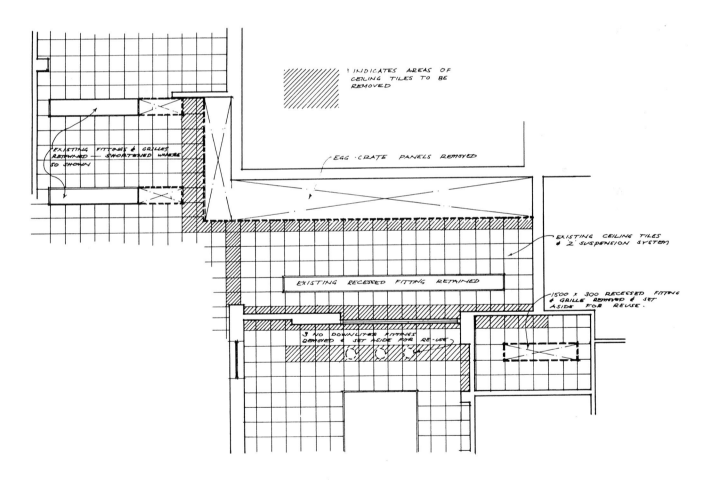

3.27 *Demolition drawing of reflected ceiling plan*

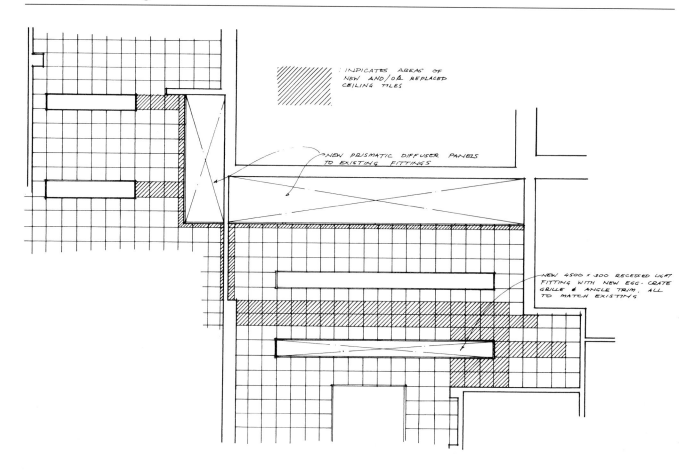

INDICATES AREAS OF NEW AND/OR REPLACED CEILING TILES

NEW PRISMATIC DIFFUSER PANELS TO EXISTING FITTINGS

NEW 4500 × 300 RECESSED LIGHT FITTING WITH NEW EGG-CRATE GRILLE & ANGLE TRIM, ALL TO MATCH EXISTING

3.28 *Drawing showing new works replacing demolitions shown in* **3.27**

from the drawings as to what is new work and what is existing. Basic structure is not too difficult to distinguish (shading in existing walls and showing the details of construction on new walls will avoid confusion in this respect) but it is the little things—manholes, rainwater pipes, sanitary fittings—often appearing as left-overs from the survey drawing, which need specific annotation.

It is, of course, helpful to issue the survey drawings as part of the set.

Activity drawings

The provision of a new door in the existing brick wall, given as an example in the section on conversions and

alterations, was an instance of an activity-oriented approach to the provision of building information. Activity 1, involving the cutting of the opening and insertion of the lintel, was rightly regarded as being distinct and of a different nature from activity 2, which embraces the fixing of a new door and frame. The two activities were separate and complete in themselves; they were potentially capable of being carried out by different people or groups of people; and they might well have been (and indeed probably were) separated from each other by a significant period of time, during which no work of any kind was being done to either the opening or the door. It was possible, therefore, and on the face of it reasonable, to convey the necessary information to the builder in the form of two separate instructions.

86

Whilst this approach to building communications is clearly sensible in the very limited context of alteration work, it is possible to apply it to the whole spectrum of building operations. Hitherto in this book a building has been looked upon as consisting of an assembly of individual elements. It may equally well be regarded as the result of a sequence of different and separately identifiable activities. Such a concept lay behind the development in the 1970s and 1980s of activity and operational bills of quantities. The theory behind them is simple. The contractor's main problem lies in the organisation of his resources, both material and human. His bricks have to arrive on site at the right time, his bricklaying force has to be sufficient to optimise the length of time his scaffolding is on hire; it must be re-deployed smoothly and economically when the work is finished, either to some other part of the project, or to another project. Success lies in careful and accurate programming.

Conventional bills of quantities do little to assist in this task. To tell the contractor that he is to erect a total of x m^2 of brick wall will enable him to put an overall price on the total brickwork/bricklayer section. It will not necessarily point out to him that the last brick will be laid some eighteen months after the first; nor that it will be laid on an entirely different part of the site; nor that the nature of the construction involves the total bricklaying operation being split into three separate stints, with substantial gaps of time between them.

Such information may well be deducible from an intelligent examination of the drawings, but the bill of quantities is, after all, the document he has to price, and were it to be presented in a form which showed the true nature of his work there would be inestimable benefits all round. The contractor would have at his disposal not only a more accurate basis for his estimating, but a flexible management tool which could be used for, among other things, the programming of material deliveries, the deployment of site labour and the forecasting of cash flow for the project. The quantity surveyor would have the advantage that remeasurement, when necessary, would be restricted to small and readily identifiable sections of the work rather than entire trade sections, and that valuations for interim certificates and final account would be greatly simplified. (It would not be a matter of agreeing how many metres of brickwork had, in fact, been erected. It would be a matter of common observation how many activities had been completed.)

The method has not become so widely established as had at one time seemed likely but it is there, readily available and consideration should be given as to whether any adjustment of working drawing technique is desirable to accompany it.

The method starts with the establishment of a notional list of building activities which, while not binding on the contractor, is nevertheless intended as a realistic attempt to put the work into a correct order. A typical sequence for a piece of brick walling, for example, might run thus:

1	Strip top soil
2	Excavate for strip footings
3	Lay concrete
4	Lay engineering bricks to DPC level
5	Lay DPC
6	Build 275 mm cavity wall to wall plate level, etc.

It is not possible for drawings to show activities, only the completed event. There is no reason, however, why an elementalised set of general arrangement drawings such as has been discussed in the previous pages should not form a perfectly satisfactory adjunct to an operational bill. In the example given, activities *1 to 3* would all be covered on the foundation plan and the remaining three on the primary elements plan. To each drawing would be added a note saying which numbered activities were shown on it (or were shown on other drawings to which that drawing referred). Against each activity in the list would be set the number of the general arrangement drawing which would initiate the search pattern.

Drawing the set

We have covered the structure of a set of working drawings, the hierarchic progression of location, assembly, component, sub-component drawings and schedules. We now have to look at how the drawings themselves are to be prepared, in a form that will be economical of drawing time and will enable multiple copies to be taken for the use of the contractor, sub-contractors, quantity surveyor and others.

There are two primary methods for producing the originals:

1 They may be created on a computer using a CAD program before being sent to a printer or plotter
2 They may be drawn manually, using pen or pencil techniques, which until a few years ago were the only options available.

Since CAD is the predominant method now in use we shall deal with it first.

Computer-Aided Draughting

At its simplest CAD is little more than an electronic drawing board. Individual drawing files are created from lines, circles and text, each file being an electronic image of the paper drawing that will be created from it. Individual lines and circles are assigned a pen width, a colour and a linetype of dashes and dots but little more than that. At the other end of the spectrum some CAD (Computer-Aided Design) programs aim to provide all the tools necessary to *design* the project, whilst all necessary construction drawings are generated automatically.

A drawing file created by CAD has the potential to be far more than just a collection of paper drawings stored on computer. Used properly, it can be a database describing a building in its entirety as a 3D model, from which plans, elevations and sections can be generated as and when needed, at any scale, and showing any sub-set of information. The drawing file would be created from walls and windows rather than lines and circles, and these walls and windows might have their size, weight, cost, materials and manufacturer details attached. The same drawing file might also be used to generate isometric or axonometric diagrams, or photo-realistic coloured perspectives. The same file might be used at all stages of design and construction, from initial proposals and discussions with the client through production information and on to 'as built' information. As the project progressed through these stages information would constantly be added to the drawing files. The client might also use them for facilities management (sometimes called asset management) once the building was handed over.

CAD possesses many advantages over manual drawing, even for a small practice. A computer takes up far less space than a drawing board, so you don't need as large an office. It can double up for writing specifications, getting information from manufacturers over the Internet or from CDs, sending and receiving messages, and even doing your accounts. You don't have to keep pens clean and pencils sharp.

A drawing created on a computer doesn't need to be built up sequentially. Mistakes can be corrected easily without starting afresh, and revisions and repetitions are easy to make. You can start on a computerised drawing even if you don't have all the information to hand to complete it, because you can come back later, make corrections and fill in details. At this level CAD has done for drawings what word processors did for text.

A good CAD package will also let you automate difficult or repetitive tasks, so that whole sections of drawings can be completed with just a couple of clicks on a button. It should either have all the necessary 'hooks' to allow links with third-party applications when you decide to add them, or have a file format compatible with architectural design packages, to make it easier to upgrade later.

Some ancillary equipment is useful. A CD or better still a DVD writer enables back up copies to be made of valuable data and copies sent through the post. An A4 flat bed scanner enables site location plans or manufacturers' trade literature to be scanned into CAD drawings. A 4 megapixel digital camera can provide a photographic record of existing buildings and topography, saving a return trip to site.

Most offices now use large format inkjet plotters capable of printing A1 or A0 drawings. Smaller offices might send small drawings and check plots to the same A4 laser printer as is used for general correspondence and send larger drawing files direct to plotting agencies over the Internet.

With regard to the actual creation of the drawing files, two methods are currently in use, the first being both the most common and the less sophisticated.

Drawing overlay method

The basic concept is simple. Each element of the design is drawn on its own unique 'layer' within the computer file, walls on one layer, dimensions on a second, electrics on a third, radiators on a fourth, and so on. Layers can be turned on or off as needed. During the design process both electric and radiator layouts might be turned on, enabling electric sockets behind radiators to be spotted.

The concept of layering is common to all CAD programs. Different programs might use different terminology but the underlying principle is the same. All programs will have tools to help you manipulate your layers, by way of wild carding or through grouping layers. Likewise, layer names might be preassigned by a high-end fully automated architectural CAD program, whereas you may have to devise your own layer naming conventions with a simpler program. (See Chapter 5 for section on Layer Naming Conventions.)

However, if in doubt, use more layers than fewer. It is much easier to combine layers to simplify the drawing file's structure than it is to separate drawn entities into two or more layers later.

Model exchange method

When drawings are produced by CAD it is probable that during the design process several different designers will work on the project at different times and on different computers. It is also possible that on more complex projects creation of the production information set will be shared between different professionals working in separate offices. The traditional method of exchanging data and coordinating various aspects of a project would have been to send marked up prints back and forth through the post, with separate sets of drawings being produced as the final design emerged.

In model exchange, where all the professionals are using CAD to produce their drawings (ideally but not necessarily the same CAD program), it is the 'model' that is sent back and forth on disk, CD or by email rather than pieces of paper through the post. Hopefully, the final scheme is better coordinated, with fewer errors, omissions and conflicts. Management procedures must be in place to ensure that everyone is working from the same version of the CAD model, but in theory at least, a better set of production information should be created, with far less duplication of effort.

Manual drawing

This has now been largely superseded by CAD. The most recent RIBA survey indicates, however, that 15 per cent of small practices still draw the bulk of their work manually, and it seems desirable therefore that some notes be included covering the method of elementalising drawings manually.

The method is very similar in essence to the CAD drawing overlay method described previously. A basic floor plan is drawn (see the section entitled 'the basic floor plan' in Chapter 2) and from it are taken the requisite number of copy negatives (normally by dyeline reproduction on some translucent medium which will take manual drawing on its top surface). The elemental information is then added to each copy negative, which is then coded elementally and printed for inclusion in the drawing set.

The use of copy negatives is really only applicable to general arrangement drawings. Even in situations where an assembly or component drawing has been given an elemental CI/SfB coded number it is unlikely to have benefited from the superimposition of additional layers of information and might as well have been produced as a single sheet, drawn once only.

Paper size is of less consequence here than in the other methods discussed, for the production of the negative is limited only by the size of the drawing board available and the cost implications of using large drawings are not so great as they are with more sophisticated methods. Nevertheless, the same general comments regarding paper sizes which were made earlier still apply with manual draughting. No one is going to think kindly of you while trying to consult an A0-sized drawing flapping about in a gale on an exposed building site.

As to the medium upon which manual drawing may be carried out, there is a wide range, coupled with a range of pens and pencils.

Materials for manual draughting

Detail paper has the great advantage of being cheap and, because it offers a semi-opaque background, pleasant and satisfying to draw on, particularly in pencil. It is best suited to the preparation of drafts for subsequent tracing into final drawings, where the original sheet may be expected to have a limited life, and where any prints taken from it will be for internal exchange of information among team members, and also for rapidly produced pencil details (accompanying architects' instructions, for example).

Tracing paper is the most common medium in use today. A smooth finish is desirable, especially for pencil work, where the more abrasive surfaces of the matt and semi-matt finishes tend to wear down pencil points rapidly and are more difficult to keep clean during the preparation of the drawing. A weight of 90 g/m^2 is probably the most common in general use but it is arguable that 112 g/m^2 justifies its extra cost, being dimensionally more stable and less liable to go brittle with age.

Draughting film is expensive but it is dimensionally stable, takes ink and pencil well and both may be erased easily. However, it is hard on the normal technical pen and it is desirable to use a range with specially hardened tips.

Ink and pencil are the two available media for drawing lines and the choice rests to some extent with the individual. Many find pencil the more sympathetic medium, with its wide range of line inflexions. The function of a working drawing, however, is the unambiguous conveyance of drawn information, and aesthetic considerations must remain secondary.

Line thickness

Line thicknesses offered by the manufacturers of technical pens cover a wide range. Figure **4.1** shows them at full size. It will be noted that there are two ranges available, Range One being the most common and Range Two based on German DIN standards. With Range Two each size doubles the thickness alternately preceding it, with the result that alterations may be carried out to an enlarged or reduced copy negative in a similar weight of line to that appearing on the original. (This applies equally when manual alterations to CAD printed drawings is being carried out.)

It is of course undesirable to mix the ranges on any given drawing. For 1:2 reduction of negatives the minimum recommended line thickness for use on the original drawing is 0.25 mm, allowing the use of the minimum size 0.13 mm pen for any alterations.

In any process of reduction the minimum line thickness on the final print should not be less than 0.13 mm if

range one	range two
Line thickness in mm	Line thickness in mm
0.1	0.13
0.15	0.18
0.2	0.25
0.3	0.35
0.4	0.5
0.5	0.7
0.6	1.0
0.8	1.4
1.2	2.0

4.1 *The range of line thicknesses available with the use of technical pens*

legibility and uniformity of reproduction are to be maintained. But for the normal production of working drawing negatives, where reproduction may be expected to be at a 1:1 ratio, there is no reason why a thickness of 0.18 or 0.2 should not be selected for the thinnest line used.

Three different line thicknesses will suffice for most drawings. If we term them (a), (b) and (c), with (a) being the thinnest and (c) the thickest, the various parts of a drawing may be grouped within them as follows:

> (a) grid lines
>
> centre lines
>
> dimension lines
>
> leader lines
>
> incidental furniture, where relevant
>
> hatching
>
> (b) all other lines, with the exception of:
>
> (c) those lines, particularly on an elementalised drawing, which it is desired to emphasise, either because they define the element which is the subject of the drawing, or in the general interest of clarity.

The values to be set against the three categories will vary with the scale and nature of the drawing and with the range of pen sizes selected.

Recommended pen sizes are as follows:					
1 Drawings to a scale of 1:50 and less	(a)	(b)	(c)		
2 Drawings to a scale of 1:20 to 1:5		(a)	(b)	(c)	
3 Drawings to a scale larger than 1:5			(a)	(b)	(c)
Pen size Range 1	0.2	0.3	0.4	0.5	0.7
Pen size Range 2	0.18	0.25	0.35	0.5	0.7

Figures **4.2** and **4.3**, taken from parts of drawings of various scales, have been redrawn using both pen size ranges for comparison.

Drawing sheet size

The international 'A' series of paper sizes is now universally accepted, and all drawing and printed sheets used in the office will conform to its requirements. It originates in the ingenious concept of a rectangle having an area of 1 m^2, the length of whose sides are in the proportion 1:$\sqrt{2}$ (**4.4**).

The dimensions of this rectangle will be found to be 1189 × 841 mm and by progressively halving the larger dimension each time, a reducing series of rectangles is produced, in which the proportions of the original rectangle remain unchanged, and in which the area of each rectangle is half that of its predecessor in the series (**4.5**).

The range of 'A' sizes available to the drawing office is as follows:

> A0: 1189 × 841 mm
>
> A1: 841 × 594 mm
>
> A2: 594 × 520 mm
>
> A3: 420 × 297 mm
>
> A4: 297 × 210 mm

CAD uses these paper sizes, with the addition on larger drawings of a gripping margin for the printer or plotter.

The large differential between A0 and A1 has led to the introduction in some offices of a bastard-sized sheet to reduce the gap, but the use of intermediate sizes is not desirable. They have to be cut from paper of a larger size, and their non-standard proportions lead to difficulties in both storage and photographic reproduction.

Indeed, both these and the A0 sheet should be avoided wherever possible. The A0 sheet is incredibly cumbersome both in the drawing office and on site, and on the whole it would seem to be preferable to set the A1 sheet as an upper limit in all but the most exceptional circumstances. The site plan for even the largest of projects can always be illustrated at the

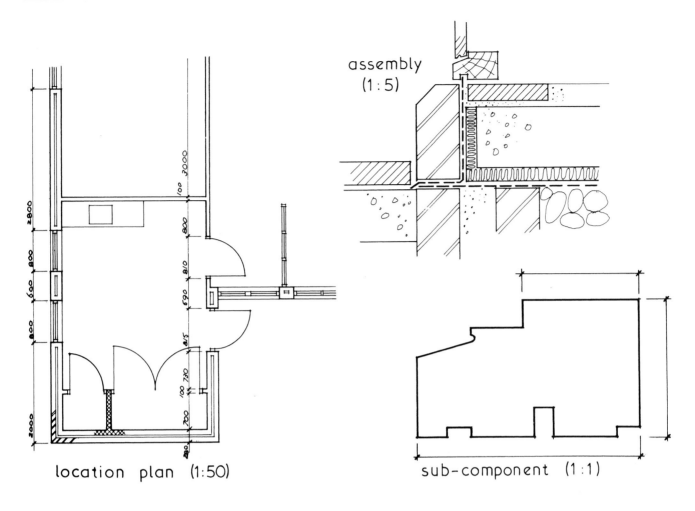

assembly
(1 : 5)

location plan (1:50)

sub-component (1 : 1)

4.2 *Parts of three drawings using the Range 1 line thicknesses*

appropriate scale on a number of marginally overlapping sheets, with, if necessary, a key sheet drawn more simply at a smaller scale to show the whole extent of the site (**4.6**).

Where an area is sub-divided in this fashion a small key plan should always form part of the title block to indicate the relationship of that particular drawing to the overall plan (**4.7**).

Apart from this upper limitation it is clearly sensible to restrict as far as possible the number of different sized drawings issued on any one project. An early appraisal

of the size of the job and of the appropriate scale for the general arrangement plans will probably establish the format for the complete set of such drawings; normally it is not difficult to contrive that the assemblies and the ranges of component drawings should also be drawn on sheets of that size. The majority of the drawings in the average set therefore will appear in either A1 or A2 format, depending upon the size of the project.

The nature of sub-component drawings and schedules however, tends to make a smaller format more suitable for them, and there will always be, in addition, a number

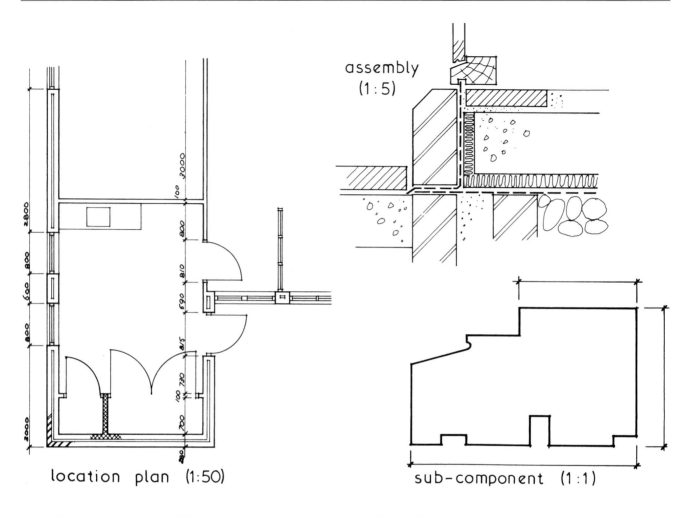

location plan (1:50)

assembly (1:5)

sub-component (1:1)

4.3 *The drawing shown in 4.2 redrawn using the recommended Range 2 line thicknesses*

of small details on any project which it would be pointless to draw in one corner of an A1 sheet and which it would be confusing to attempt to collect together on a single sheet (the 'miscellaneous details' approach which has been condemned earlier).

Where the format for the other drawings is A2 it is probably worth wasting a little paper for the sake of obtaining a manageable set of consistent size. Where the general size is A1 however, a smaller sheet becomes necessary and whether this should be A4 or A3 is a matter for some debate.

A4 or A3? It may be helpful to set out the pros and cons. The advantages of the A4 format are:

• A substantial amount of the project information is already in A4 format—specification, bills of quantities, architect's instructions, correspondence, etc.
• Trade literature is normally A4 and if you wish to include manufacturers' catalogues as part of your set (and why not?) then they are more readily absorbed into the structure of the set if you already have an A4 category.

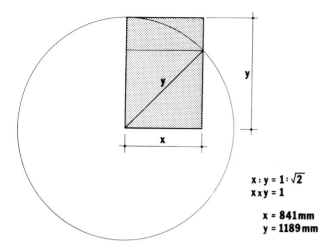

$$x:y = 1:\sqrt{2}$$
$$x \times y = 1$$
$$x = 841\,mm$$
$$y = 1189\,mm$$

4.4 *Derivation of the rectangle A0, with a surface area of 1 m²*

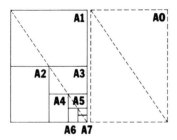

4.5 *'A' sizes retain the same proportions (1:√2). Each sheet is half the size of its predecessor*

- Most users—both producer and recipient—will possess or have access to an A4 photocopier with the facility that this offers to, for example, the contractor who wishes to get alternative quotes for a particular item and can rapidly produce his own copies of the particular drawing. The A3 copier is still something of an expensive rarity (though their use in contractors' and professional offices is becoming more common).
- The restricted size of sheet makes it more suitable for producing standard drawings, where it is necessary to limit the amount and extent of the information shown in order to preserve its 'neutrality'.

- Architects' instructions are frequently accompanied by a sketch detail and the A4 format simplifies filing and retrieval.
- A bound set of A4 drawings is suitable for shelf storage. A3s are an inconvenient size to store, whether on a shelf, in a plan chest drawer, or in a vertifile.
- A4s can be carried around easily.

The disadvantages of the A4 format are:

- The drawing area is altogether too small. One is constantly being forced into the position of limiting what is shown because there is just not room on the paper, or of selecting an inappropriately small scale.
- There is no room to record amendments adequately, or for that matter to incorporate a reasonably informative title panel.
- Builders don't like them.

The choice is not easy but on the whole the authors are inclined to favour A3 as the smallest sheet of a set, if only for the pragmatic reason that you can, at a pinch, hang them landscape in a vertifile; that you can, at a pinch, bind them into a specification or a bill of quantities and fold them double; that you can, at a pinch, copy them in two halves on an electro-static copier and sellotape the two halves together; and that wasting paper is, in the last resort, cheaper than redrawing a detail which in the end just would not quite go on the sheet.

Drawing conventions

In the same way that line thickness is influenced by considerations of scale and the relative importance of the objects delineated, so too is the degree of detail by which various elements are represented. The manner in which a door or a window is shown on a 1:20 assembly drawing is not necessarily appropriate to their representation on a 1:100 general arrangement plan.

As always, common sense and absolute clarity of expression are the criteria. If a door frame is detailed

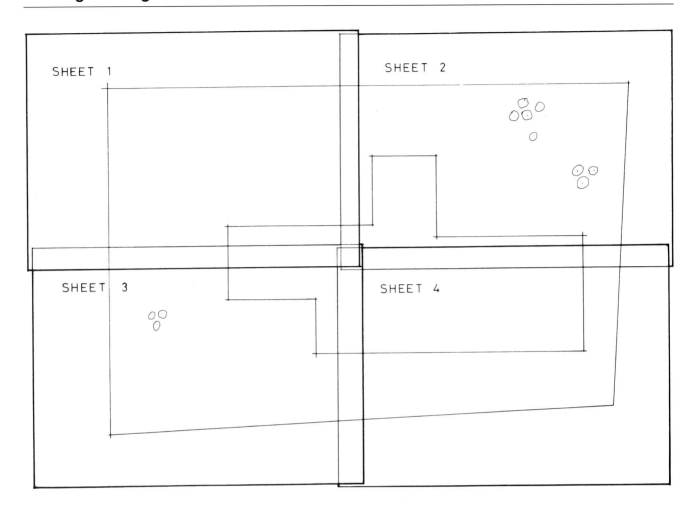

4.6 *Overlapping smaller sheets allow the appropriate scale to be used for the plan of a large area without recourse to unwieldy A0 sheets*

elsewhere in the set at a scale large enough for the intricacies of its moulding to be described accurately, then it is a waste of time and a possible source of confusion if an attempt is made to reproduce the mouldings on a 1:20 assembly drawing whose real function is to indicate the frame's position in relation to the wall in which it sits.

Some conventional methods of representation which are generally speaking appropriate for a range of elements at various scales are given in Appendix 1.

Handing and opening The conventions for describing the side on which a door is hung are many and varied. These are sometimes ambiguous, at worst contradictory, and few areas where precise description is vital suffer so much in practice from imprecision as this one.

Possibly the simplest and most easily remembered convention is this: that the hand of an opening is the side on which the hinges may be seen. (BSI's 'clockwise closing' and 'anti-clockwise closing' cut across long engrained terminology.)

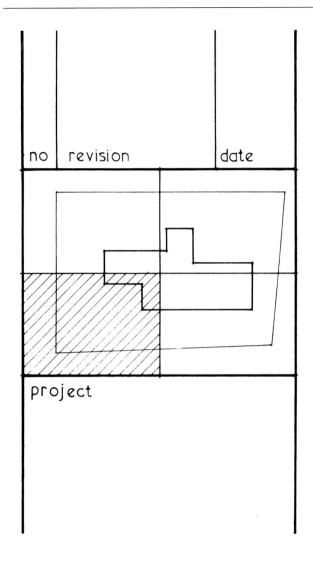

4.7 *Key to sub-divided plan forms part of the title block*

The use of this convention provides a ready mental reference for checking the handing of any component and for providing instructions to others. Like any other convention, however, it is of little use to the recipient unless they are in on the secret. So they must be told, preferably by a simple statement at the start of the component schedules.

The conventions determining window openings are in more general use, presumably through the early development of the metal window industry with its requirements for off-site hanging of casements and a consequent clear system for describing the handing.

The normally accepted convention is that the window is drawn as viewed from the outside. Conventional representations for both door and window openings are given in Appendix 2.

Hatching   The use of hatching of various kinds to give a graphical indication of different materials was first developed as a readily reproducible alternative to the laborious colouring of opaque originals which had preceded it.

The existing ranges of conventions are based on building techniques of a previous century, and were they to be brought fully up to date an enormous expansion of conventions would be necessary. Such concepts as loose-fill insulation, for example, fibre-glass mouldings, or glass-reinforced cement would all require consideration.

One should first question the necessity, or indeed the desirability, of hatching in the first place. It should only be used when confusion is likely to occur in the interpretation of drawings, and in most cases such potential confusion may be avoided by other means. Building elements shown in section, for example, may be distinguished from lines in elevation or grid lines by affording each their proper line thickness, without recourse to hatching. Different materials are less likely to be confused with one another when drawings are elementalised; and in any case, the mere differentiation between, say, brickwork and blockwork, which is possible with hatching, is not normally sufficiently precise for present-day purposes. We want to know if the bricks are commons, or engineering quality, or facings. We want to know if the blockwork is lightweight for insulating purposes or dense and load-bearing. Such subtleties can only be covered by proper annotation and such annotation will often render other methods redundant.

Where hatching is used it should be kept simple in convention. Often a simple diagonal hatching, with the diagonals running in different directions, will suffice to illustrate the function of two components of the same material, without requiring that the user look up some vast code book to see what the material is. This is clarified in the accompanying notes.

Gridded hatching, where the grid is parallel to the axes of the element being hatched, is confusing to interpret.

The foregoing comments apply equally to hatching applied during CAD draughting, even though such hatching is simple and rapid to apply.

Some conventions in common use, simplified from their original sources, are given in Appendix 3 but their use should be very much conditioned by the comments above.

Electrical symbols

The architect frequently becomes involved in the production of electrical layout drawings, particularly on smaller projects where no M & E consultant is engaged, and Appendix 4 gives some of the more commonly used symbols in general practice.

Two points may usefully be made about the method of showing wiring links between switch and fitting. In the first place, of course, any such representation on the drawing is purely diagrammatic; no attempt need be made to indicate the precise route the wiring should take. (If ducted provision has been made the fact should be noted on the drawing and the ducting shown on the appropriate builder's work drawing.)

In the second place, the links are far better drawn curved than in straight lines which are liable to conflict with other building elements (see **2.7** in Chapter 2).

Non-active lines

Lines on a drawing which delineate the actual building fabric are termed 'active lines'. Those lines which are essential to our understanding of the drawing, such as grid lines, dimension lines, direction arrows, etc. are termed 'non-active' lines.

Recommended conventions for non-active lines are given in Appendix 5.

Templates

Various plastic cut-out templates are on the market, covering many of the symbols given in the appendices. Templates are also available for the production of circles and ellipses and for drawing sanitary fittings.

Such templates are a time-saving aid, even though one of the corollaries of Murphy's law ensures that the symbol you really need is missing from that particular template. A word of warning should be added about the indiscriminate use of templates for sanitary fittings, where it is dangerously easy to fool yourself about dimensions. Some manufacturers of sanitary fittings produce their own templates, and these of course give an accurate representation of the particular fitting specified. However, in their absence it is safer to draw the fitting to its true overall dimensions taken from the manufacturer's catalogue than to rely on a standard template which may deceive you into a situation where the toilet door fouls the lavatory basin which arrived on site larger than you had drawn it. Figure **4.8** gives an example of a typical template.

Block libraries (templates)

The CAD equivalent of drawing templates is the block library.

Dedicated architectural CAD programs will come complete with their own 2D and 3D block and symbol libraries. These programs will allow you to select

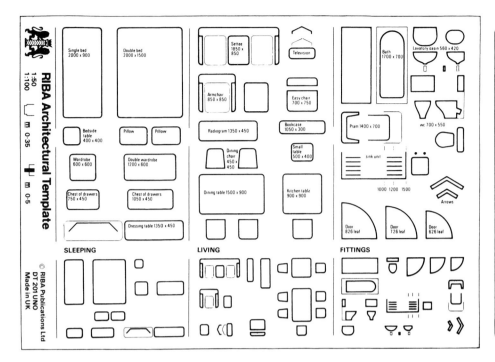
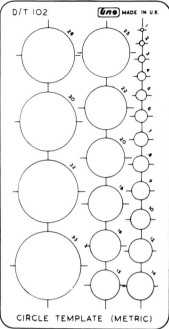

4.8 *Examples of plastic cut-out templates available commercially*

symbols or component drawings from menus and insert them in your drawings where needed. The more sophisticated programs will add the inserted components to automatically generated schedules.

Several generic block and symbol libraries are available for sale, some with CAD versions of diagrams from books that you can insert straight into your drawing files. These are designed to give you some of the benefits of dedicated architectural packages at a much lower cost (**4.9**).

One long-term aim of the building industry is that manufacturers start to provide libraries of intelligent 'objects' rather than simple blocks. The task is immense and although the dedicated architectural CAD programs already use 'objects' it seems unlikely that we shall see any substantial number of 'object' libraries in the near future.

The final source of block and component libraries is to create your own. A not inconsiderable advantage of creating your own libraries is that quality is ensured. A disadvantage with some low cost libraries is that they were produced, seemingly, by very junior staff and not checked thoroughly before distribution. At least you know your own libraries are perfect.

It is not necessarily an onerous task to create these libraries. They can be built up over the years by 'writing out' parts of drawings you create for use later on other projects.

Dimensioning

That this is a more complex subject than may appear at first sight may be illustrated by a simple example.

Consider a timber window set in a prepared opening in an external wall. Unless the wall is to be built up around the window frame, in which case the frame itself will

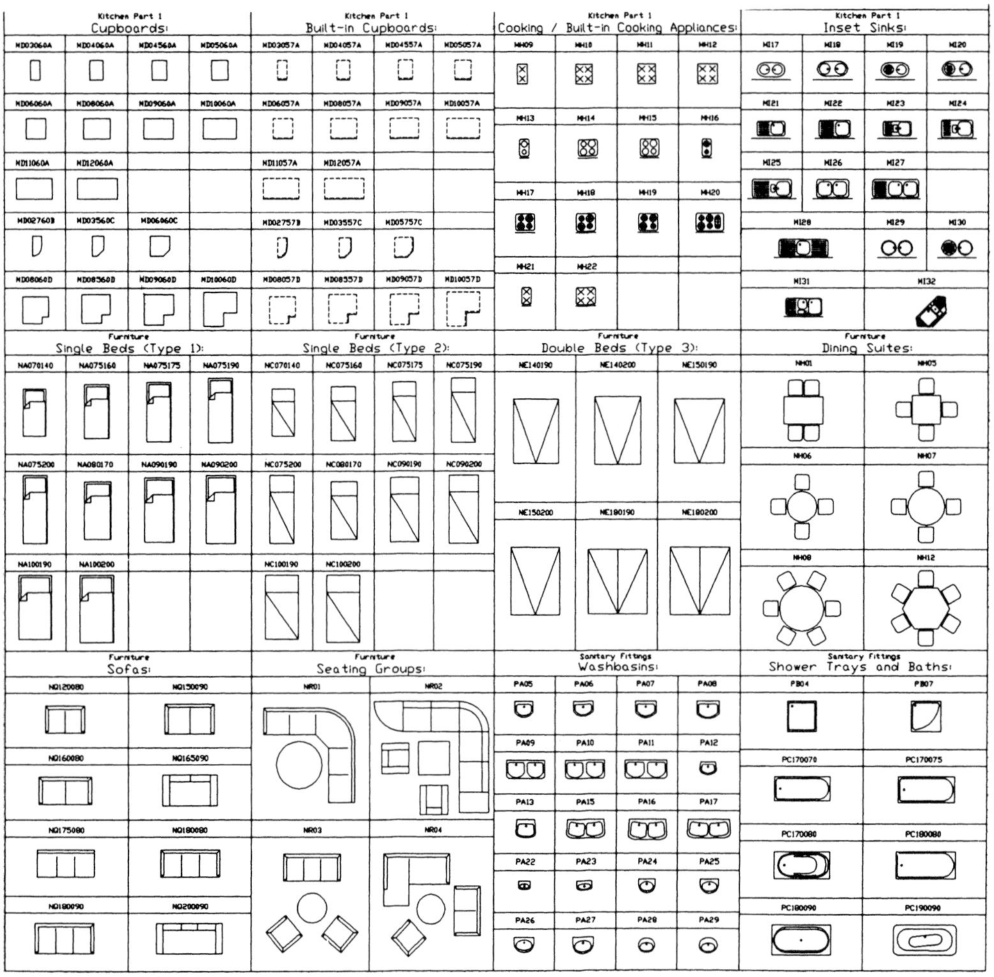

4.9 *The conventions shown are contained in computer software and may be selected as required for the drawing being undertaken. (Reproduced by courtesy of Autodesk Ltd)*

serve as a template for the opening, the architect will be faced with making the brick opening larger all round than the overall dimensions of the frame which is to be fitted into it; for otherwise it will be impossible, in practical terms, to insert the one into the other. It would seem that the joiner will need to work to one set of dimensions and the bricklayer to another if a satisfactory fit is to be achieved. How, simply, is each to be instructed?

To answer 'dimension the frame 15 mm all round smaller than the opening' is unduly simplistic. Apart from the

daunting prospect of trying to represent a series of 15 mm differences on a general arrangement plan at a scale of 1:100, the problem is compounded by inaccuracies which are bound to occur in both the fabrication of the frames and the erection of the brickwork, to say nothing of the difficulty of inserting one centrally into the other.

The solution lies in the concept of the coordinating dimension, which may be defined as the distance between two hypothetical planes of reference—known

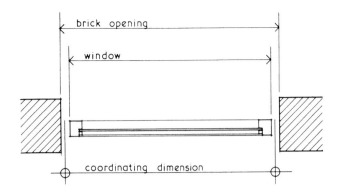

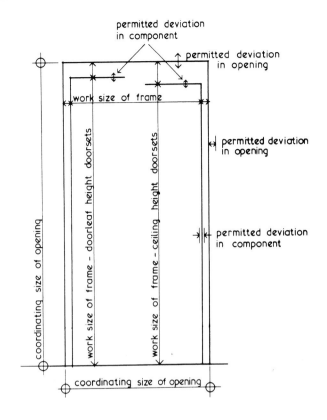

4.10 *The coordinating dimension*

4.11 *The work size*

as coordinating planes—representing the theoretical boundary between adjoining building elements. A diagrammatic indication of the window in the wall will clarify this definition (**4.10**).

The coordinating dimension is the one which will be shown on the general arrangement and assembly drawings, and is the nominal dimension to which both the bricklayer and joiner will work. If that dimension is 1500 mm, then we may speak quite properly of a '1500 opening' and of a '1500 window'. The nominal size of the frames will be reduced by the manufacturer to a size which is smaller all round by 10 mm, this being the dimension laid down by the British Woodworking Manufacturers' Association as an appropriate reduction for timber products in order to produce a final or 'work size'.

We now have a situation which may be shown diagrammatically as in **4.11**.

It must be borne in mind, however, that neither the bricklayer nor the joiner is likely to achieve 100 per cent dimensional accuracy and the best that can be done is to specify the degree of inaccuracy that will be regarded as acceptable.

In the present example two trades are involved, and the degree of precision to be demanded must be realistically

related to the nature of the materials in which each is working. It may be assumed that the bricklayer will set up a temporary timber framework as a simple template to which this brickwork may be built to form the opening. For the bricklayer therefore, an opening which varies in size between $x + 5$ mm and $x - 0$ mm with x being the coordinating dimension may be considered reasonable. In the timber component however, it will be reasonable to accept variation in size between $y + 5$ mm and $y - 5$ mm where y is the laid down work size of the component.

The final assembly of window and brickwork may therefore have two extreme dimensional situations, with a range of intermediate possibilities (**4.12**).

The selected method of sealing the gap between component and opening must take account of these variables if it is to work in all situations. The sizing of

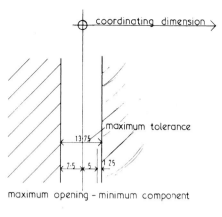

maximum opening – minimum component

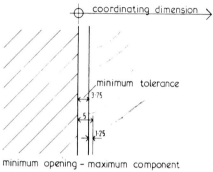

minimum opening – maximum component

4.12 *Dimensional possibilities of window/wall assemblies*

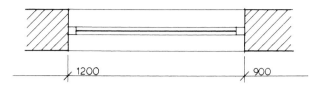

4.13 *Opening on plan defined by its coordinating dimension*

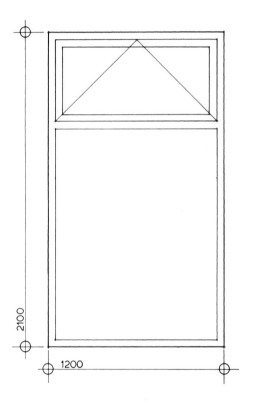

4.14 *Component destined to fill the opening shown in **4.13** is also defined by its coordinating dimension*

components and the establishment of their work sizes and permitted deviations is an entire field for study in its own right. An obvious instance is that of pre-cast concrete cladding panels with a compressible extruded plastic section providing the weathertight seal between them where, unless the greatest care is taken, the maximum permitted gap between panels may be too great to hold the plastic section in compression, while the minimum permitted gap is too small for it to be inserted. The UK Building Research Establishment's paper on 'Tolerance and Fit' is important reading in this connection, as is BSI's 1999 publication BS EN ISO 6284.

The above discussion is intended as the most basic of introductions to a complex subject. But it may be seen how the whole of dimensioning practice becomes simplified by the concept of the coordinating dimension.

The assembly of window and wall will be dimensioned on the general arrangement plan as in **4.13**, and if he is wise, the architect will similarly designate the coordinating dimensions on the component drawing (**4.14**).

It will be prudent to note in the drawing set that this method has been adopted. A note on the component schedule or component drawing stating that 'Dimensions given for components are coordinating dimensions. The manufacturer is to make his own reductions to give the work size of the component' should avoid the possibility of error.

Definitions

It may be helpful at this point to summarise some of the terms referred to in a list of definitions and to add to them others in common use:

Coordinating plane: Line representing the hypothetical boundary between two adjoining building elements.

Coordinating dimension: The distance between two coordinating planes.

Controlling dimension: The key dimension—normally between coordinating planes—which is the crucial determining dimension in an assembly and which must remain sacrosanct while intermediate dimensions may be permitted some tolerance.

Work size: The actual finished size of a component.

Permitted deviation (sometimes known as manufacturer's tolerance): The amount (plus or minus) by which the finished size of a component may vary from its stated work size and still be acceptable.

Dimension line: The line drawn between two planes with a view to showing the dimension between them.

Extension line: The line drawn from a plane which is to be dimensioned and intersecting the dimension line.

Leader line: The line joining a note with the object which is the subject of that note.

Some examples

Appendix 5, dealing with non-active lines, gives examples of the types of dimension line recommended for different purposes.

The following comments may be helpful in establishing the correct approach to dimensioning such diverse drawings as the site plan, primary element general arrangement plans, general arrangement and assembly sections, and component and sub-component details.

To set out a building it is necessary to establish a datum parallel to one of the building's axes. The criteria by which this datum is selected will vary. Where there is an improvement line required for the site, or an established building line, these will obviously be important starting points. If the site is relatively uncluttered then existing physical features—boundary fencing, adjoining buildings, etc.—will be used. In certain specialised structures orientation may well be the overriding factor.

The important thing is that the chosen starting points should be unambiguous and clearly recognisable on site.

It is better to establish the datum some distance from the perimeter of the new building so that it may be pegged in as a permanent record during construction. The building may then be set out from it by offsets. A datum which coincides with one of the new building's faces will be obliterated as soon as excavation starts.

Where the construction is load-bearing the setting-out dimensions from the datum should be given to the outside face of the wall. Where the structure is framed this dimension should be to grid centre-lines.

The dimensioning of the plan shown in **4.15** is largely self-explanatory. Note the three strips of dimensions along the external walls, the string picking up the grid being the outermost line of the three. Overall dimensions are included, partly as an arithmetical check for the dimensioner, partly to aid the estimator.

Generally speaking, internal setting out is effected by judiciously selected strings of dimensions. Where the

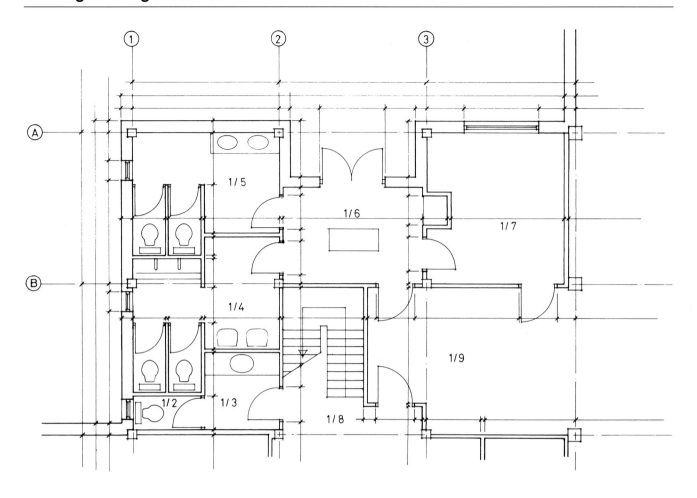

4.15 *Typical dimensioning of general arrangement primary elements plan. (The other general arrangement plans in the set will not need to record these dimensions)*

positioning of a given element is critical however (where, for example, it must be a precise distance from a certain wall face), it will be dimensioned from that face alone, to ensure that the setter-out works in a similar fashion. When it is critical that a feature be in the centre of a wall face an 'equal/equal' indication should be given from its centre line.

Figures **4.16** and **4.17** show the role of the controlling dimension in vertical setting out. The salient levels dimensioned from the relevant datum (in this case the finished floor level) in the assembly section appear again as reference planes in the larger scale detail.

The only comment that needs to be made about components and sub-components is the general one, that they should be dimensioned to their finished sizes.

This is particularly relevant when the material involved is timber. A note to the effect that the finished section is to be 'ex 150 × 150' is too imprecise for a constructional world of off-site fabrication. Economy requires that the finished section should realistically be obtainable from one of the standard sawn sections. To give a *finished* size of 150 × 150, for example, would result in the client paying for a large quantity of wood-shavings and sawdust.

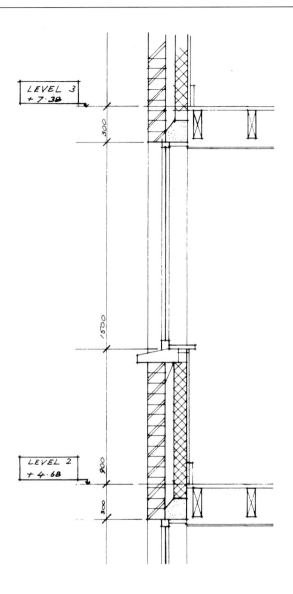

LEVEL 3
+ 7·38

LEVEL 2
+ 4·68

4.16 *The controlling dimension*

Grids

The use of shadow grids has been around for a long time, particularly among the manufacturers of building systems, where components tend to be modular and junctions simple and standardised. They are applicable to traditional building as well however, whenever a modular discipline exists, and when used with discretion can speed up the production of drawings and reduce the need for elaborate dimensioning.

The superimposition of grids presents no problem with CAD, as they can be assigned their own unique layering that can be turned on and off at will.

When drawn manually grids may be combined with the use of pre-printed sheets. A half-tone is usually adopted for the printing of the grid itself, appearing on the finished print in a fainter line than those used for the rest of the drawing. In practical terms, the use of grids is limited to general arrangement plans and they are of the greatest benefit in projects where rationalisation of the design has restricted the size and position of the elements. In **4.18** for example, where the use of a grid of 6 mm squares has allowed each square to represent a 300 mm module at a scale of 1:50, the placing of the 100 mm partition has been limited to one of three conditions. It is either centred on a grid line, centred on a line midway between grid lines or has one face coinciding with a grid line. Similarly, the door frame, with a coordinating dimension of 900 mm, is always situated so that it occupies three entire grids.

No dimensions are needed to locate such elements if the discipline for positioning them is established from the outset and is known to everyone using the drawings.

A word of warning however. It is not realistic to expect the man on site to set out a wall by counting grids and doing his own calculations. Dimensions should always be added to the grid for key setting-out positions, overall lengths and controlling dimensions.

Title panels

The title panel should be at the bottom right hand corner of the sheet, so that when the drawing is folded properly, the title and number are always clearly visible. A possible exception to this is when A2, A3 and A4 sheets are being used, where the title panel might be reduced in height and spread across the full paper width to provide a more useable drawing area.

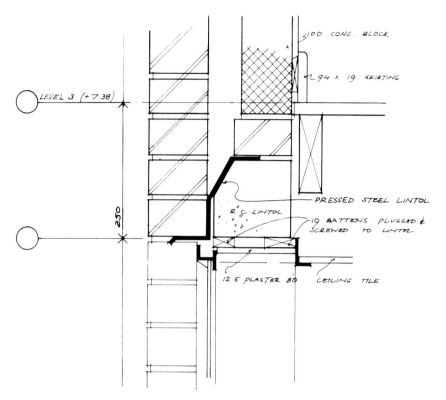

LEVEL 3 (+7·38)

250

5100 CONC. BLOCK

94 × 19 SKIRTING

PRESSED STEEL LINTOL

R.C. LINTOL

19 BATTENS PLUGGED &
SCREWED TO LINTOL

12·5 PLASTER BD   CEILING TILE

4.17 *Vertical location of elements in the assembly section is given by references to the planes established in 4.16*

Figure **4.19** shows the recommended method of folding various 'A'-sized sheets.

The format of the panel will vary but it must make provision for the following (minimum) information to be displayed:

Name and address of the project
Name, address, telephone number and email address of
   the issuing office
Title of the drawing
Scale of the drawing
Coded number of the drawing (status of issuing office—
   e.g. architect, structural engineer, etc.; nature of
   drawing—e.g. general arrangement, assembly, etc.;
   CI/SfB code, and unique number in that series
Date of first issue
Reference, description and dates of subsequent revisions.

The panel may carry further optional information, such as the name of the project architect, the names of the persons preparing and checking the drawing, office job reference, etc.

Figure **4.20** shows a suitable format; however, many are available.

Title panels when drawings are prepared manually are best pre-printed on to standard drawing sheets. When the drawings are CAD-produced however, the panel is prepared electronically. It should be defined as a CAD block and inserted into each drawing sheet, which can then in turn be inserted into every drawing on the computer.

If your practice logo uses a specific font it is probably best to create a bitmap image of that logo (.tif or .bmp) and insert that into your title panel. (See Glossary of CAD terms.) That way the logo will not change if the computer used for plotting the drawing (such as a plotting agency) does not have that font installed.

Depending on your CAD program it may be possible to link the text items in the title panel into a database or to CAD software to maintain a drawing register automatically and keep track of revisions and drawing issue (see additional notes on managing the set in Chapter 5.)

When drawings are prepared manually trimming lines and margins is unnecessary when standard 'A' size

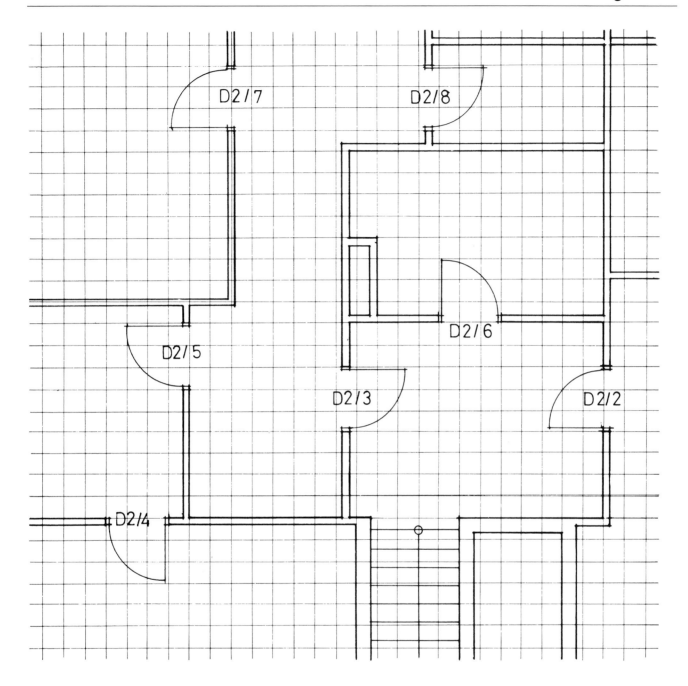

4.18 *Modular discipline eliminates the need for complicated dimensioning by limiting the location of elements to certain standard situations. (Scale of original 1:50)*

sheets are used. It is useful however, if the line marking the left-hand of the title panel continues up for the full extent of the sheet, since this reserves a strip along the side of the sheet for the addition of notes, revisions, etc.

In CAD usage each drawing sheet should include a border so that you can see where the edges of your paper will be when creating the drawing in the computer. (If the border is on its own layer it can be turned off

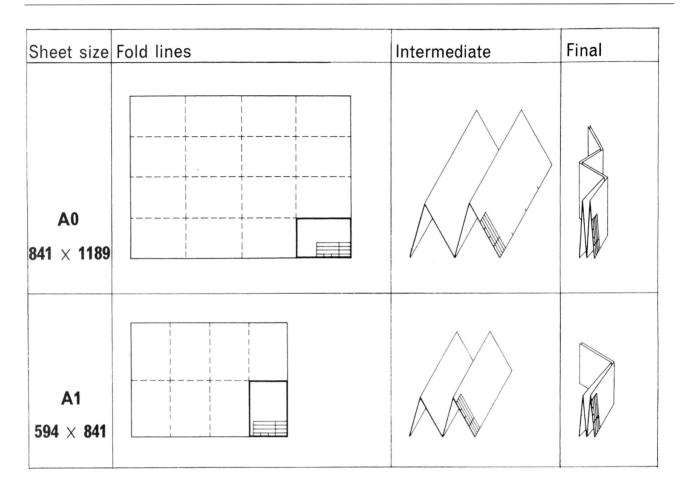

Sheet size	Fold lines	Intermediate	Final
A0 **841 × 1189**			
A1 **594 × 841**			

4.19   *Recommended method of folding 'A'-sized sheets always keeps the title panel visible*

before printing if you prefer.) But many printers and plotters need margins at the edges to hold the paper firm as it passes through the machine, so the borders should be placed to take account of these. If you are using a plotting agency don't forget to set up sheets to suit their plotter too.

When completing the title panel it is most important that the drawing title be stated simply and consistently, giving the casual searcher a brief but accurate and informative statement about the drawing's content:

Arch/ G/ level 1/ (21)/ 027

We are told, in sequence, that the drawing is prepared by the architect; that it is a general arrangement; that it is a plan taken at level one; and because this is an elementalised set of drawings, we are told the element which the drawing shows, i.e. primary element dealing with walls. 027 is the drawing number in that series.

The identical title will appear in the drawing register (see Chapter 5).

Annotation of the drawing

Adding text to a drawing presents few problems when working with CAD. Modern CAD programs, connected to

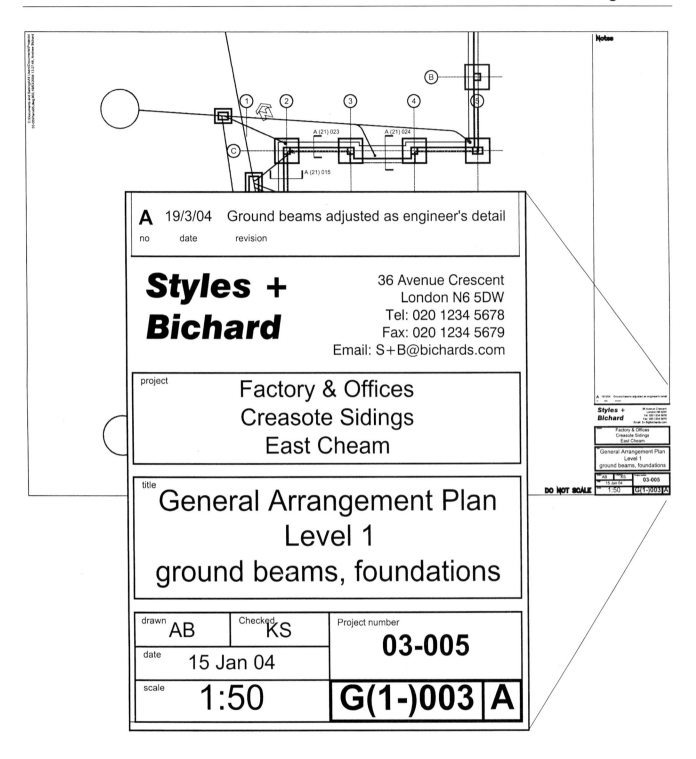

4.20 *Example of drawing title panel*

laser printers or inkjet printers, will have access to all the fonts installed on the operating system. There is a huge choice of styles, any of which might be used for text notes in the drawing. But remember that the aim of text is to convey information clearly and concisely. Don't go overboard with too wild a font style and do use a size that is big enough to read on site. Imagine that a bricklayer with dirty hands is trying to read the drawing in the rain before the paper tears.

Use one of the more common fonts, so that the text looks the same whatever computer you use for plotting. (If the font used to create text in the drawing isn't installed on the computer that is used for plotting, the computer will attempt to substitute its best guess of close match for you, with sometimes surprising results!)

Arial is a simple and legible font and is widely used. Text on CAD-produced drawings in this book has been annotated in Arial.

Hand lettering

With the pre-eminence of CAD this tends to be a dying skill. But even in the fully automated office there is from time to time the need for a manually prepared and lettered drawing, if only to provide the site office with an urgently needed detail. Such occasions demand a lettering style which is both rapid and legible.

Figure **4.21** shows a recommended sequence of strokes in the formation of individual upper case letters. Increasing fluency and self-confidence (each generates the other) will enable this stroke-making procedure to be simplified in due course into an acceptable and rapidly produced individual style. Horizontal guide lines are beneficial and if they are in blue pencil they will not appear on the subsequently produced dyeline print.

Lettering for general annotation should be a minimum of 2 mm in height for upper case letters and 1.5 mm for

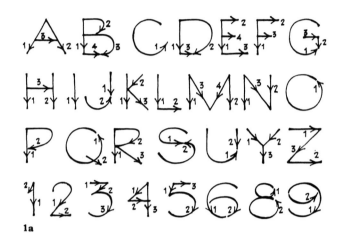

CLEAR LETTERING CAN BE PRODUCED AS EASILY AND AS SWIFTLY AS SCRATCHY LETTERS, BY USING THE CORRECT TECHNIQUES:

1. FORM EACH CHARACTER USING THE CORRECT SEQUENCE OF SEPARATE, SIMPLE STROKES.

2. HOLD THE PEN AT AN ANGLE OF 45° TO THE LINE OF WRITING IF IT HAS A FLAT NIB. HOLD PEN/PENCIL UPRIGHT.

3. WITH PEN & INK, USE LEAST POSSIBLE PRESSURE: NEVER PRESS ON NIB.

4. PRACTICE AT FIRST USING HORIZONTAL AND VERTICAL GUIDELINES. THEN, AFTER LETTER FORMATION HAS BEEN MASTERED, USE GRIDDED SHEET UNDERLAY UNDER TRACING PAPER AS GUIDE.

4.21 *Formation of the upper case alphabet*

lower case. The spacing between lines of upper case letters should not be less than the lettering itself. With lower case lettering the space should be somewhat greater than the lettering to allow for upstanding stems and tails.

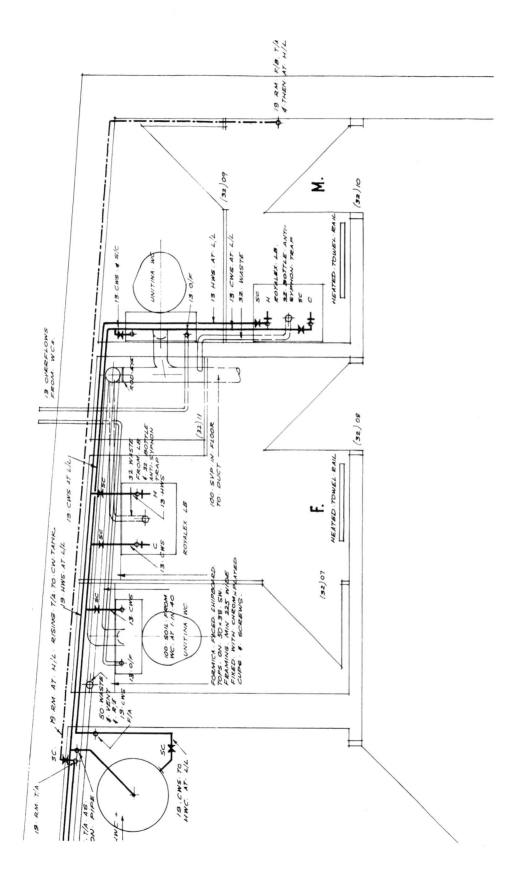

4.22 A well-annotated plan (original scale 1:20)

The line should be either 0.3 mm or 0.25 mm, depending on which range of pen sizes is being used.

Most lettering will normally run from left to right of the drawing, parallel to the bottom edge of the sheet. Should it become necessary for lettering to run vertically it should always run from the bottom upwards. (This applies equally to dimensions.)

With lower case lettering the spacing should be somewhat greater than the lettering size to avoid upstanding stems from one line coming into contact with the tails from the line above.

Figure **4.22**, prepared manually, is an example of well-spaced out lettering on a quite complex detail (actually a (52) general arrangement plan showing the drainage services). Note how a little forethought at all stages in the production of this plan has helped to ensure that notes, dimensions and coded references do not clash with each other or with the building.

Working drawing management

The objective

Prior to this chapter production information has been the primary concern. It is this information—both drawings and specification—which represents the final commitment to the building project of planning and constructional decisions arrived at during the earlier stages. This documentation is inevitably a time-consuming process and if it is to be carried through smoothly and economically it is important that all the necessary decisions should have been taken before its commencement.

It is also true to say that of all the aspects of an architect's work it is this final documentation that lends itself best to the deployment of a team. On very few projects will there be the time available to allow the working drawings to be prepared by a single individual and in practice quite small buildings will involve more than one person at this stage.

The objective therefore, is the achievement of a rapid, well-programmed set of drawings, in which the information to be documented by each member of the team is allocated in advance with due reference to his experience and ability, and during which only the most routine and undemanding of technical problems should remain for resolution. In order to achieve this it is important that a more or less rigid adherence to the plan of work is maintained.

The plan of work

The RIBA Plan of Work was illustrated in Chapter 1 as constituting the basic discipline within which the manifold activities of the architect are contained. Against each stage were noted the major aspects of work dealt with at that stage which will have a bearing on the working drawing process or which will be influenced by it.

The plan of work is sometimes criticised as being doctrinarian and unrelated to the harsh facts of professional life. Certainly, in practice there are constant pressures to do things out of sequence because there is a short-term benefit to be gained by doing so. It is very tempting when struggling with knotty problems of detailing or seemingly lethargic fellow consultants, to take the view that a premature start on the final drawings will in some way have a cathartic effect on the enterprise.

The increasing use of CAD, of course, has blurred the separation of the various work stages described in the plan of work. In the same way that word processing has transformed writing, CAD has transformed the process of designing buildings and describing them through working drawings. The process is no longer a strictly linear one. We don't necessarily have to finish the design before we start on the production information (though we may well be unwise to do so.)

CAD forces the designer into making some decisions far earlier than might otherwise have been the case. Even at outline stage it is possible for the walls to be drawn with absolute accuracy, taking account of brick, block and cavity thicknesses; openings may be drawn to conform with coordinated brick dimensions. The layout might change as the design evolves but at any given moment in time the 'model' is accurate.

Nevertheless, a proper laying of the groundwork will help to avoid those drawing office crises, destructive alike of morale and financial budgeting, when a team of several people is brought to a standstill by the sudden realisation of some unresolved problem. So from the standpoint of stage F let us look back to the preceding stages, where a little forethought will make life in the subsequent stages a great deal easier.

Pre-requisites for stage F

There is a basic minimum of information which needs to be available before embarking on stage F and this should certainly include the following:

---

final set of design drawings (stage D)
record of statutory approvals (stages D and E)
key detailing in draught (stage E)
room data sheets (stages C to E)
outline specification

---

applicable trade literature
library of standard details
drawing register
design team network
drawing office programme

These items are dealt with in detail below.

Final design set (stage D)

It will always be necessary to produce a set of drawings showing the final design, and if subsequent changes are called for, no matter how minor, it is sensible to record these on the drawings or CAD files themselves in addition to any other form, so that at any one time there exists an up-to-date record and confirmation of what has been agreed with the client.

Obviously these will be presentation drawings, prepared in the manner best calculated to obtain the client's approval. Nevertheless, before the trees and the shadows are added, it is prudent to take a set from the unadorned master files, for then definitive plans and elevations will be available which may be issued immediately to other consultants on commencement of stage E, and the rather fruitless business often encountered of 'draft working drawings' once design approval has been obtained may be eliminated, with benefit to both office economics and programme.

This implies, of course, that the scales and draughting techniques should be compatible with use for both purposes but this is quite feasible if their subsequent use is borne in mind from the outset (**5.1** and **5.2**).

The use of CAD, of course, renders the whole process much simpler and of even more economic benefit. The final design plans, denuded of their extraneous trees and shadows, will serve directly as the basic file for subsequent elementalisation, with the decorative

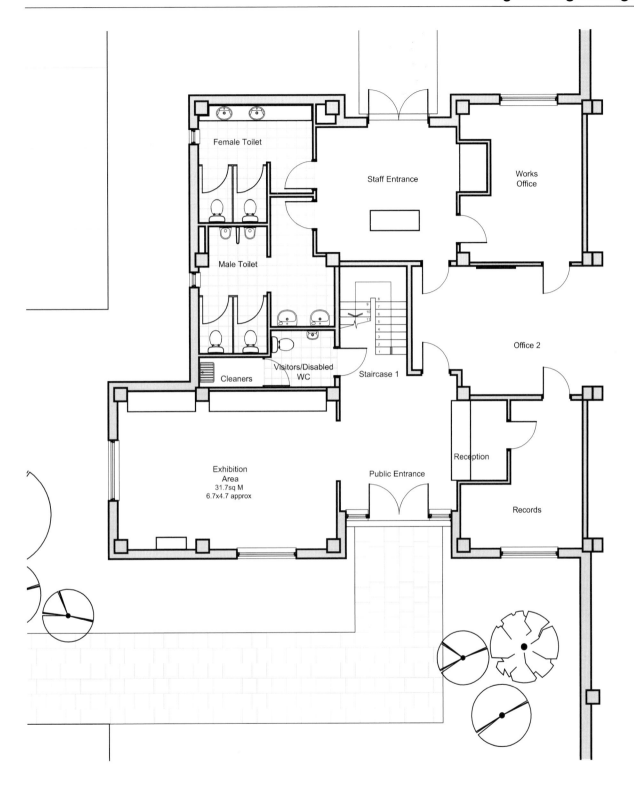

5.1 *Final design drawing as issued to the client for approval. Presentation techniques are designed to display the scheme attractively and to assist a layman's understanding of it*

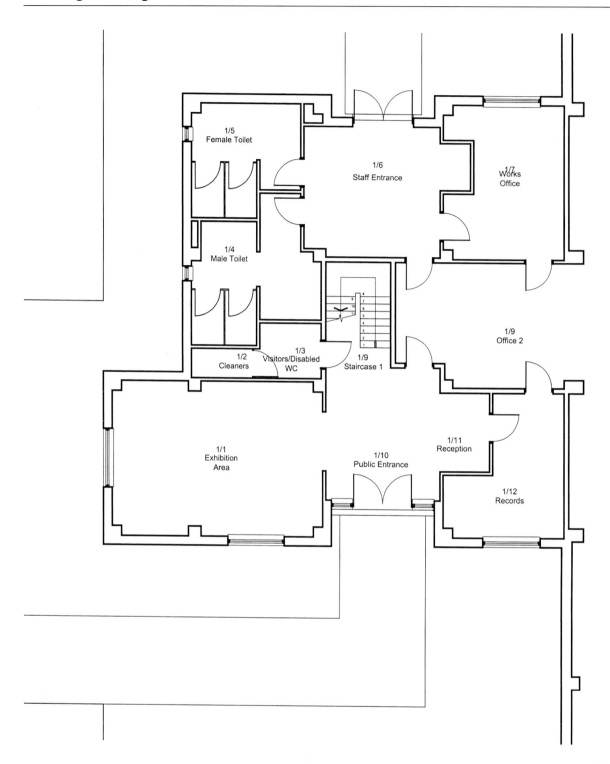

5.2 *Copy taken from **5.1** before the blandishments were added. Scale and simple draughting make it suitable for issue to consultants for preparation of their own scheme drawings (or to nominated sub-contractors when CAD is not being used)*

presentation features possibly remaining as an invisible layer in the set.

Statutory approvals

A chicken and egg situation this one—you can't get approval until you've submitted the drawing: it's pointless preparing the drawing until you've got approval. But visits to the fire officer and the building inspector in the early stages of the scheme will not only set up lines of communication which will be invaluable for the future but will establish principles for incorporation in subsequent detailing. It is a firming-up process. It is essential to know at the start of stage C the spacing of escape stairs the fire officer will demand and by the end of it their widths. It is essential to know before the end of stage E the required fire rating of all doors. Nobody should need to raise such questions in the middle of stage F.

The decisions and agreements must be recorded, of course, and it is obviously more helpful to give someone a marked-up drawing to work from than a bulky file to read. The final design drawings referred to above as being issued to consultants form an obvious basis for the recording of this sort of information (**5.3**).

Key detailing in draft (stage E)

At the completion of stage E there should be a carefully thought out solution available for every construction problem that can be envisaged; this will involve the production of a sheaf of draft details in which the principles of these solutions are established.

The drafts will not be elaborated into final drawings. They will remain as source documents and the decisions they embody will be fed out into various stage F drawings—or computer files if CAD is being used for detailing. General arrangement sections, assemblies and component details, as well as the specification, will come into this category.

It should be noted in particular how one draft assembly section generates a whole series of detailed statements about various aspects of the building. In the past it might have been thought adequate to issue the section as a final drawing, a 'typical section' from which the operative might be expected to infer detailed variations to suit differing but basically similar situations throughout the building. In today's very different conditions this is just not adequate.

It is, however, reasonable to expect a drawing office assistant to apply the principles involved to other aspects of the building, which they will either identify or which will be identified for them by others with greater experience or knowledge of the particular building.

This approach to detailing, whereby the basic principles of construction are established by the principal or the project architect but are translated into detailed practice by an assistant, lends itself to considerable drawing office economies. By defining the necessary drawing office tasks at the outset of the programme (a subject which will be dealt with in detail later) the appropriate level of responsibility may be set for all members of the team.

Room data sheets

The advantages of room-by-room scheduling as a medium for conveying information about internal finishes and fittings have been noted earlier. The gradual collection during stage E of such information into a source document of comparable format will clearly assist in the preparation of such schedules at stage F. Whether this is done on a copy of the floor plan or on a series of individual sheets representing each room or room type, is a decision which will be made in the light of the size and complexity of the individual project. At the end of the day there will exist, hopefully, a complete record of each room's requirements, with indications where applicable as to the authority for those requirements, serving alike as a detailed record of client instructions and a briefing manual and check list when the final document is being prepared (**5.3**).

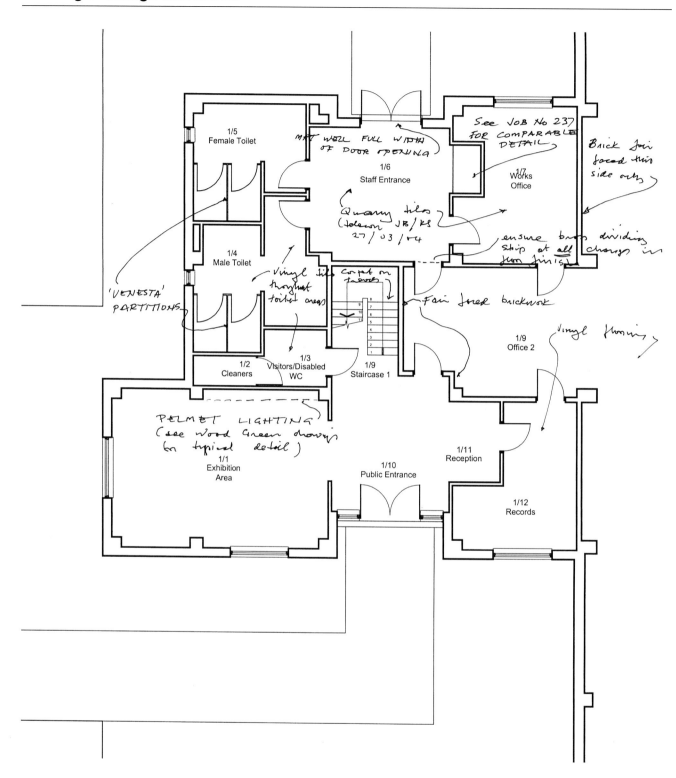

5.3 *Copy taken from **5.2** and marked up as a briefing guide to the drawing office at stage E*

Outline specification

The case is argued elsewhere in this handbook for a specification which is an integral part of the production documentation rather than the afterthought which puzzled site staff often assume it to have been. If drawings are to be freed of the detailed written descriptions they are frequently made to carry, it is implicit that this information must be conveyed to the contractor by other means. Indeed, the philosophy of the National Building Specification is reliant upon the geometry of the building and of its component parts being covered by the drawings, with selection from alternative materials and definition of quality standards being covered by the specification.

It should be noted that some CAD programs specifically tailored for architects will provide links to NBS specifications. It can also be helpful to have both a CAD drawing and NBS text file open at the same time on a computer, with the designer preparing the specification in parallel with the drawings.

It is desirable therefore that both drawings and specification should draw their information from a common source document and that this document should be produced before the stage F programme gets under way.

The outline specification is a useful format for this document, partly because something approaching it will have been needed by the quantity surveyor for his final design stage cost check to have any validity.

It consists basically of a check list (CI/SfB elemental order is a convenient framework) upon which decisions of construction and materials may be noted as they are made.

Formalising these decisions into such a document at an early stage ensures that they are made at the proper level of experience. Readers of *The Honeywood File* will recall Ridoppo, the wonder paint that crept off the walls and out of the house. We have all had our Ridoppos but at least it ought to be possible to ensure that they are not selected by the drawing office junior at the last minute because time was short and nobody had told him any better.

Trade literature

The rationalised drawing structure provides a convenient framework on which to hang manufacturers' literature. There is no virtue in redrawing the builders' work details printed in Bloggs & Company's catalogue when a photocopy or scanned image suitably overcoded with the job and drawing number will convey the information more cheaply and accurately. (Bloggs & Company are not likely to object to the resultant wider distribution of their literature.) Indeed, a number of manufacturers will provide the architect with CDs of their products, for incorporation into their CAD drawings.

Manufacturers' trade literature should always be reproduced with caution. If there is an error in the manufacturers' literature and this is reproduced in the architect's own drawing, who is responsible if a manufacturer corrects an error in a data-sheet but the architect does not update his drawing based on that data-sheet – who is liable?

However, in any case the literature which it is known will be required, if only as source documents for one's own drawings, should be assembled early in the day. It can be frustrating to interrupt work on a detail to telephone for urgently needed trade literature and then wait two or three days for its arrival (**5.4**).

Library of standard details

Many practices attempt, at some point in their existence, to crystallise the accumulated wisdom and experience of the practice into a set of standard details, only to find with increasing disillusionment as they proceed, that not nearly so much is really standard as was at first supposed, and that the very existence of a standard drawing which is nearly (but not quite) applicable to the project in hand is a dangerous inducement to compromise.

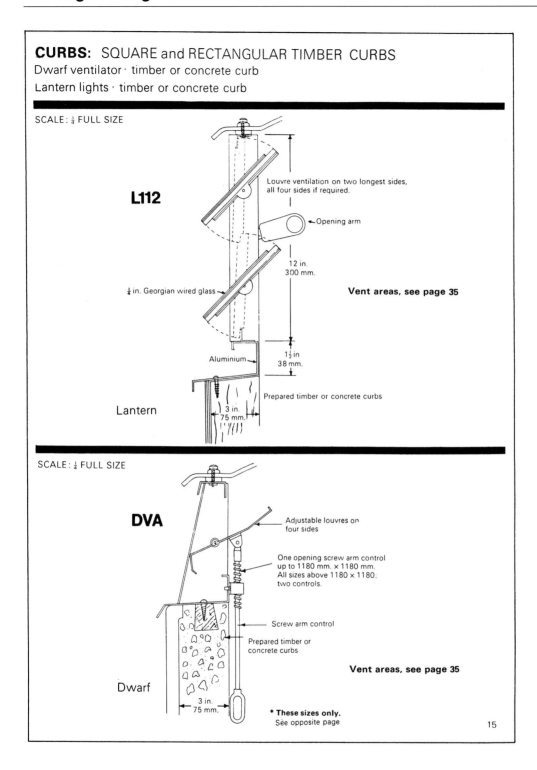

CURBS: SQUARE and RECTANGULAR TIMBER CURBS

Dwarf ventilator · timber or concrete curb

Lantern lights · timber or concrete curb

SCALE: ¼ FULL SIZE

L112

Louvre ventilation on two longest sides, all four sides if required.

←Opening arm

12 in. 300 mm.

¼ in. Georgian wired glass →

Vent areas, see page 35

Aluminium →

1½ in 38 mm.

Prepared timber or concrete curbs

Lantern

3 in. 75 mm.

SCALE: ¼ FULL SIZE

DVA

Adjustable louvres on four sides

One opening screw arm control up to 1180 mm. × 1180 mm. All sizes above 1180 × 1180; two controls.

Screw arm control

Prepared timber or concrete curbs

Vent areas, see page 35

Dwarf

3 in. 75 mm.

* **These sizes only.** See opposite page

15

5.4 *Manufacturer's catalogue gives precise fixing details. It is pointless to redraw this information when the catalogue can be issued to the contractor as an instruction*

On the other hand, it is frustrating to realise that the detail being worked out laboriously in one room on project A is not going to end up significantly different from the detail simultaneously being worked up across the corridor for project B. There should be room somewhere for a common-sense approach which does not attempt too much.

In practice, few assembly details can be drawn so 'neutrally' as to render them directly reusable on more than one project. The best that can be achieved in this field is to collect together drawings for various projects which embody solutions to recurring problems of principle, making them available for reference rather than direct reuse. The ease with which details drawn with CAD from another project can be altered and reused makes them ideal candidates for an office's standard vocabulary.

Component drawings are another matter, however, and provided that the office is using a structured drawing method it should be possible for each project to contribute its quota of contractor-made components (there is no point in redrawing proprietary items) to a central library. Such components as doorsets, shelving, cupboard fitments and external works items—bollards, fencing, etc.—are suitable subjects for treatment.

The details, once selected for a standard library, should sensibly be renumbered to ensure that when reused on new projects they do not conflict with the numbering sequence for that project. C(32)501, for example, might well be the first drawing in a library of internal joinery components, and would not conflict with component details specific to the project and numbered C(32)001, etc.

The use of CAD raises other issues. The ease with which details stored electronically may be altered means that assembly drawings too may more frequently form part of a standard vocabulary.

Design team programme

It is essential for the work of the entire design team to be integrated into a comprehensive programme, and unless a specialist programmer forms part of the team (and this is almost a *sine qua non* for any very large or complex project) then the management role of team coordinator falls to the architect. Of all the consultant team an architect is probably best fitted by virtue of his training and other duties to exercise the skills required, and should take advantage of his position as team leader to establish the appropriate procedures at the outset (see the section Design team meeting).

In setting down the programme on paper, it will be found that a simple network is the best format, where the dependencies of the various team members upon each other may need to be shown. The format suggested in an early (but still valid) edition of the *RIBA Management Handbook Guide on Resource Control* is a good way to do it (**5.5**).

Its complexity may be unnecessarily daunting for the small- to medium-sized project however, particularly when a non-technical client is involved (the method is best suited to computer analysis and critical path method which may not always be available). A simplified version on which a time scale has been superimposed will serve the same purpose in most cases (**5.6**).

The point to be re-iterated is that every job, no matter how small, benefits from thoughtful programming, and the things to watch which are common to any method you use are:

Restrict the network to as few activities as you reasonably can, paying particular attention to those activities whose completion is a prerequisite for subsequent action by others. The purpose of the network is to provide each member of the team with basic management information. (Each team member may well wish to develop, for their

Work analysis: Precedence diagram

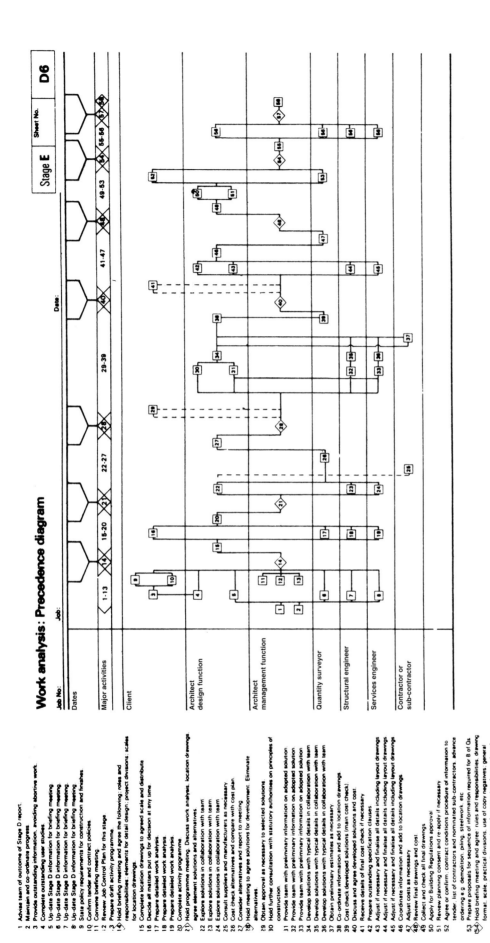

5.5 *Precedence diagram (taken from an early edition of the RIBA Management Handbook). It has the advantage that it offers a rapid assessment of the consequences of any programme's change, by its compatibility with computer analysis*

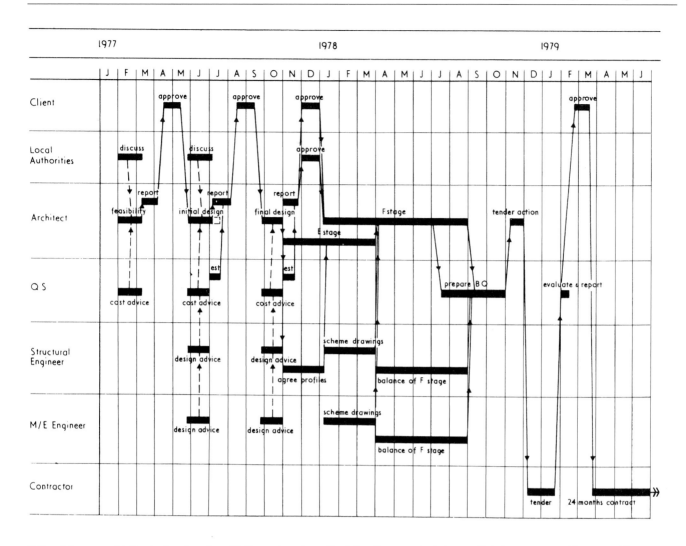

5.6 *A less sophisticated network, with the advantage that the time scale is immediately apparent. More readily understandable by the average client (and architect?) than a computer print out*

own purposes, a more detailed network of their own activities within the team management's framework.)

Make it simple. Its value as a document is that it can respond rapidly to a changed situation, and it must always be a realistic statement of the current position if it is to retain its credibility. It is no use having a programme drawn so beautifully and in so much detail that no one has the heart to redraw it when it becomes out of date.

Involve the client. Many of the client's activities are critical ones, particularly his formal approvals at various stages in the design, and he must be made aware of his responsibilities at the outset, along with the other members of the design team. In so far as his approval may be conditional on consideration by committees within his own organisation adequate time for decision-making must be built into the programme.

Planning the set

The structure of the final production set of drawings is central to both the smooth running of the project on site and the economics of the office producing it. It must therefore be considered in some detail.

General arrangement plans

Given that the set is to be structured in the manner recommended in the earlier chapters the first decision to be made (and as noted earlier it will have been sensible to make it before preparation of the final design drawings) relates to sheet size and scale of the general arrangement plans. Basically the choice lies between a scale of 1:50, permitting a relatively large amount of information to be conveyed on a single sheet, or 1:100 where a greater degree of elementalisation will be required if the sheet is to remain uncluttered and legible, and where its main purpose is to provide a ready indication of where other and more detailed information is to be found.

A number of considerations will determine this decision, but they will centre around the size and complexity of the project. Housing and conversions are normally best carried out at the larger scale. Larger projects are often better suited to an elementalised set of general arrangement plans.

Most CAD programmes work at 1:1. This means that the CAD 'model' is created full size, and that only later will views of this 'model' be created, and only then that the drawings will be assigned their plotted scale. It is obviously important that every drawing be presented at a recognisable scale in general use in the building industry.

In the discussion that follows it will be assumed that a single multi-storeyed building of some £2 000 000 contract value is being dealt with (the building, in fact, parts of which have been used previously in Chapters 1 and 2), that a drawing team of three or four people will be involved, and that the decision has been made to produce 1:100 general arrangement plans, elementalised for clarity.

Assuming that the set is to be produced by CAD, the first allocation of files will be to general arrangement plans, one for each plan level. They will be coded G(——) i.e. 'The project in general', because they are the basis from which the subsequent elementalised layers will be produced. (As has been noted in Chapter 4, numbering of the plans by floor levels is a refinement which, apart from possessing a certain elegance for the system-minded, offers eventual benefits to the site staff).

The basic plans having been established it is necessary to consider what elemental plans should spring from them. The CI/SfB project manual offers a sensible method for identifying these. The complete range of elements in CI/SfB Table 1 is available and offers a useful check list (see Chapter 1).

Generally speaking, however, few projects—and then only those containing problems of a specialised nature—will need to go beyond the much more limited range shown in Table IV.

Other general arrangement drawings

Site plan, elevations and basic sections complete the general arrangement set. The complexity of the external works will influence the decision on whether or not to put all general arrangement information on a single drawing. This is an area where coordination of information is of paramount importance and this may outweigh the other advantages inherent in the elemental approach.

General arrangement sections

These are best identified from the final design drawings. The external envelope of the building will generate the majority and the most important of these, so the approach illustrated in **5.7** is useful. Bearing in mind that the approach initially is in terms of strictly limited

Table IV   A typical range of CI/SfB codes used on a large project

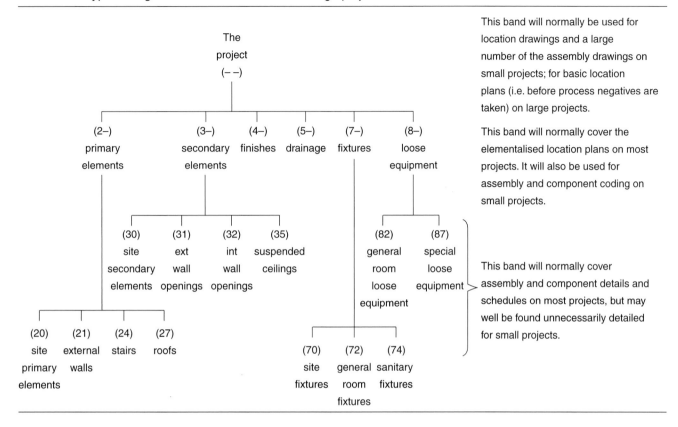

This band will normally be used for location drawings and a large number of the assembly drawings on small projects; for basic location plans (i.e. before process negatives are taken) on large projects.

This band will normally cover the elementalised location plans on most projects. It will also be used for assembly and component coding on small projects.

This band will normally cover assembly and component details and schedules on most projects, but may well be found unnecessarily detailed for small projects.

strip sections rather than the traditional 'section through the building', work systematically round the building, marking on a print the necessity for a fresh section every time the condition changes. You will finish with a series of G(21) details—desirably at a scale of 1:50—whose function will be to establish all important vertical dimensions and to provide references to larger scale (and largely repetitive) assembly details of head, sill and eaves, etc.

The general arrangement drawings are listed in Table V as they would appear in the drawing register.

Assemblies, components and schedules

The assembly drawings, component drawings and schedules appropriate to a project of this nature are listed in Table VI.

The drawing register

The drawing register is a key document in the proper organisation of a working drawing project and as such needs to be something rather more than the loose sheet of paper with a scribbled list of drawing numbers and titles which sometimes suffices. After all, it serves a multitude of purposes, being at various times a declaration of intent, a record of performance and, in the event of dispute on abandonment of the project after commencement of the working drawings, possibly a legal document.

In any case, it will have a relatively long and hard life, so it should be housed in a hardback folder or file, preferably of a colour striking enough to make it easily identifiable in the drawing office (it is essential that it be to hand immediately whenever a drawing is completed)

125

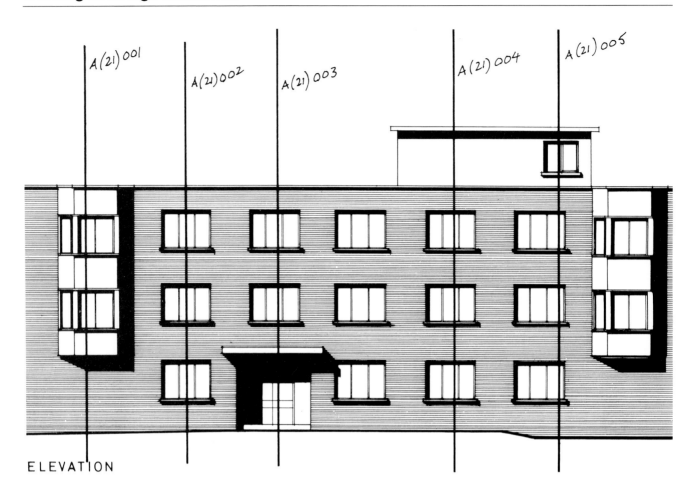

A(21)001 A(21)002 A(21)003 A(21)004 A(21)005

E L E VAT I O N

5.7   *A print of the elevation has been used to identify every section through the external walls where the construction changes*

and in a loose leaf format so that sheets may be removed and inserted easily. A4 is the obvious size, and **5.8** illustrates a useful format.

It is strongly recommended that the register be prepared at the beginning of the working drawing programme, immediately the approximate list of required drawings has been identified. Its sequence of entries, therefore, will be similar to that of the hypothetical list of drawings and schedules given in Tables V and VI; that is to say, it will be divided into general arrangement, assembly, component and schedule categories, and a single sheet will be given to

each CI/SfB element used. In consequence, there will be a relatively large number of sheets in the register, but the advantage will be that the bones of the drawing structure are laid out for all to see, in strict numerical sequence, and that if subsequently the need for a fresh drawing is identified (and the initial identification is unlikely to be accurate to within 5 per cent) then it may be entered without disruption either of the drawing numbering sequence or of the register's own page order.

Within this framework the make-up of the individual register sheet may vary, but the information it should

126

Table V   General arrangement drawings listed as they would appear in the drawing register

Drawing number	Scale	Title	Comments
G(——)001 002 003 004 005	1:100	Plan at level 1—Basic 2— ,, 3— ,, 4— ,, 5— ,,	These are the basic floor plans from which copy negatives will be taken for development by the architect and other consultants into elemental plans. Numbering of plans by levels aids retrieval of elementalised information and offers a useful framework for identifying scheduled components, e.g. (31)2/11, identifies external (window) opening no. 11 on level 2. These plans in their basic form will not be issued for construction purposes.
G(——)006—009 010—013	1:100 1:100	Elevations 6,7,8,9—Basic Sections 10,11,12,13—Basic	Similar basic drawings of elevations and sections. Composite drawing numbering, e.g. 006–009, enables unique identification of each of several drawings on the same sheet. E.g. the second elevation may be referred to simply as G (——) 007, rather than 'detail no. 2 on drawing G (——) 006'. Sections are skeletal only and confined to giving a datum for each of the plan levels and giving a general picture only to the contractor.
G(——)014	1:200	Site plan	The site plan is the only G (——) drawing to contain elemental information and to be issued for construction purposes, although the G(——) elevation and sections will be issued for the contractor's background information.
G(2—)001 002 003 004 005	1:100	Plan at level 1—Primary elements 2— ,, 3— ,, 4— ,, 5— ,,	The key set of plans giving dimensioned setting out information about the building. Note that while it would have been quite possible and perfectly in accordance with CI/SfB logic to split the information carried on these (2–) plans into (21) external walls, (22)—internal walls, (23)—floors, (24)—stairs, (27)—roof and (28)—frame, common sense and the straightforward nature of the project suggested that a single (2–) grouping of these elements would suffice.
G(2—)015—020	1:50	General arrangement sections—External walls	The key a sections described earlier. They could equally well be coded (21) since they deal specifically with the external walls, but in either case their numbering commences at 15 to preserve the integrity of the numbering system. Again, 'Drawing G(2–) 015–020' provides a unique identification for each section.

Table V   (continued)

Drawing number	Scale	Title	Comments
G(3–)001	1:100	Plan at level 1—Secondary elements	This series is used in this particular set as a means of locating, and uniquely identifying for scheduling purposes, internal doors, roof lights, gulleys and balustrades. While the plans group all this information under the (3–) code, nevertheless the referencing of individual components will be more specific, e.g. plans G(3–), will locate and identify both (32) 2/007 (internal opening, i.e. door number 7 on level 2) and (34) 003 (balustrade number 3). External openings, i.e. windows, external doors, ventilation grilles, etc. are located and numbered on these elevations.
002		2— ,,	
003		3— ,,	
004		4— ,,	
005		5— ,,	
G(3–)006–009	1:00	Elevations 6,7,8,9—Secondary elements	
			Note that while suspended ceiling (35) may also be included on the G(3–) series if required it may be less confusing to give them a separate (35) series of plans. Again common sense will dictate the approach.
G(4–)001	1:100	Plan at level 1—Finishes	There are many ways of indicating the finishes you want. You may tabulate them into a purely descriptive schedule. You may code them into a form of shorthand (e.g. F3 = Floor finish type 3) and refer them back from the plans to a vocabulary of finishes. (This is the method assumed in this
002			
003			
004			
005			
G(4–)006–009	1:100 finishes	Elevations 6,7,8,9—External	set. It has the advantage that a drawn vehicle for the information already exists, i.e. the basic plans, and the elemental method allows decisions on finishes to be deferred without detriment to other more urgent information being conveyed to the contractor at the right time.) Or you may use the room data sheets already referred to, with the advantage that this approach is more consistent with the room-by-room way in which finishing tradesmen actually work.

The elevations are an obvious medium for conveying information about external finishes, and their representation may vary from Letratone to laboriously drawn brick coursing. NBS offers a more precise and less onerous alternative with its system of coded references tied back to comprehensive specification descriptions, F11/1 for example will be uniquely designated in the specifications as 'the selected facing brick laid in 1:1:6 cement-lime-sand mortar in Flemish Bond and with flush pointing' and the coding F11/1 on the elevation will delineate the areas to which this description applies.

Table V (continued)

Drawing number	Scale	Title	Comments
G(7–)001	1:100	Plan at level 1—Fixtures	Self-explanatory, although it might be questioned what
002		2— ,,	fixtures would appear on level 5 (roof). In this case,
003		3— ,,	the (7–) coding was used to cover window cleaning
004		4— ,,	track. And a flag pole.
005		5— ,,	
G(8–)001	1:100	Plan at level 1—Loose equipment	This coding seems to cover a multitude of omissions
002		2— ,,	in practice. Mirrors, notice boards, fire exit signs, fire
003		3— ,,	extinguishers—all tend to get added late in the life of
004		4— ,,	a project. Rather than re-issuing cluttered-up and
005		5— ,,	dog-earned amended copies of other plans, it is
			preferable to reserve an (8–) set of copy negatives
			for eventual use.

provide will consist of, at the minimum:

1 *Drawing category*: i.e. general arrangement, assembly, component or schedule.
2 *Drawing element*: its CI/SfB number, or other coded reference.
3 *Drawing number*: its unique identification within the category and element.
4 *Revision suffix*.
5 *Scale*: not essential to the record but can be helpful.
6 *Size of sheet*: because A4 and A1 drawings are unlikely to be stored in the same container, and the searcher must be told where to look. One test of the effectiveness of a drawing retrieval system is that it should always be quicker to locate the given drawing in the register and then go to it straight away than to leaf hopefully through the vertifile.

The date of completion and the dates of any revisions are not included, for they will be recorded on the drawings themselves. Neither is it desirable to use the drawing register as a record of drawing issues. In the first place this practice imposes an administrative strain upon the drawing office, which is likely to act unfavourably to seemingly bureaucratic procedures. In the second place, there is really very little to be gained from such a record. A check on drawing issues should be possible from other in-built procedures, such as standard drawing circulation lists or drawing issue sheets.

A CAD user would almost certainly maintain the drawing register in electronic format as a computer file.

Status coding

As has been noted earlier, many drawings perform different functions at different stages in their life, and some system of identifying their function at a given moment is a useful adjunct to a coding system.

One such method is to use the letter reference of the appropriate RIBA stage of work in conjunction with the drawing number, as follows:

E: *Detail design drawing*. Any working drawing up to the time it is frozen for issue to the quantity surveyor, when it becomes:

G: *Drawing reconciled with bills of quantities*. That is the stage at which the drawings form part of a tender set.

Table VI Assembly drawings, component drawings and schedules listed as they would appear in the drawing register

Drawing number	Scale	Title	Comments
A (21) 001–020	1:5	External wall details	Assembly details illustrating the entire range of different external wall conditions to be found on the project, including door and window heads and sills, and, in this instance, the footing, and ground floor junctions. It would have been equally possible to code these latter conditions A(16)—Foundations, or A (23)—Floors, but these were only two variants on this particular project and common sense prompted their inclusion in the A(21) series rather than a pointless further extension of the elementalisation.
A (27) 001–003	1:5	Eaves details	Parapet and eaves details, however, are covered separately under an A(27)—Roof series, largely because the office possessed a standard parapet assembly drawing which it wished to use on this project, and which was already coded as A(27). It is numbered 501 because it is desirable to keep the sequence of standard drawing numbers well clear of numbers used for specific project purposes. The gaps in numbers which thus appear may be criticised as leading to confusion and doubts on site as to whether they are in possession of the complete set. It is felt, however, that the advantages outweigh these possible objections, and that the objections themselves largely disappear if the drawing register procedures discussed elsewhere are adopted.
A (27) 501	1:5	Parapet detail	
A (31) 001–010	1:5	External wall opening assemblies—Sheet 1	The A(21) series will have covered a number of assemblies which also convey information about secondary elements—e.g. a lot of the head and sill conditions for windows and external doors. The process of filling in external openings schedules in the format recommended previously will automatically throw up a number of conditions not taken care of in this series and these, together with the jamb conditions, form the subject of the A(31) assemblies.
A (31) 011–018	1:5	External wall opening assemblies—Sheet 2	
A (32) 001–006	1:5	Internal wall opening assemblies—Sheet 1	A similar series covering internal openings. Two A1 sheets have been assumed, but the details might equally well have been carried out on a larger number of A4 or A3 sheets. Note that this series conveys assembly information only about the openings themselves—head, jambs and sills where appropriate. Information about what goes in the openings—e.g. internal doorsets—is given elsewhere in a series of C(32) component drawings. Here again, the necessity for a particular detail will be made apparent by the openings schedule.
A (32) 007–012	1:5	Internal wall opening assemblies—Sheet 2	
A (35) 001–004	1:5	Suspended ceiling assemblies	Manufacturers' drawings will often be sufficient for describing the fixing of suspended ceilings. In the present case the drawing covered the timber framework for bulkheads at changes in the ceiling level.
A (37) 001–003	1:5	Rooflight assemblies	With the limited elementalisation applied to this set, it may be argued that this drawing could have been grouped under (27)—Roofs, a category which already exists for other purposes.

Table VI (continued)

	Scale	Title	Comments
Component and sub-component drawings*			
Drawing number			
C (31) 001—008	1:20	External openings component 1 to 8	The windows and external doors in this set are conveyed on separate sheets, each sheet giving dimensioned elevation of what is required. They are supplemented by an SC(31) series of details showing
SC (31) 301–304	1:5	Sub-component construction details—Sheet 1	constructional details of the components themselves (timber sections, throatings, fixing of glazing beads, etc.).
SC (31) 305–308	1:5	Sub-component construction details—Sheet 2	As with the assemblies, where a 500 series was used to keep standard drawings separate from the project numbering sequence, here the 300 series is used for a similar purpose.
SC (31) 309–312	1:5	Sub-component construction details—Sheet 3	
C (32) 001 to C (32) 015	1:20 / 1:20	Internal openings component 1 to Internal openings component 15	Components filling internal openings covered by a similar method. The component is regarded as the doorset, rather than the door. This is in line with modern joinery shop practice and avoids the difficulties of some
SC (32) 501–504	1:5	Sub-component construction details—Sheet 1	joinery drawing methods where the door and its frame are treated as separately detailed items, giving rise to problems of coordination and of
SC (32) 505–508	1:5	Sub-component construction details—Sheet 2	dimensional tolerances. In the present method these problems are placed where they rightly belong, with the manufacturer.
SC (32) 509–512	1:5	Sub-component construction details—Sheet 3	The component construction details are in a 500 series, being office standard drawings. This is an area that lends itself profitably to
SC (32) 513–516	1:5	Sub-component construction details—Sheet 4	standardisation. The overall size of component is specific to the project, but the frame sections are standard regardless of component size.
Schedules			
Schedule number			
S (31) 001		Schedule of external openings	When the number of components in a category is small, and/or the
S (31) 101		Schedule of external ironmongery	number of ways in which potentially they may vary is also small, then it
S (31) 001		Schedule of external openings	may be left to the appropriate location drawing to identify them, and to
S (31) 101		Schedule of external ironmongery	the appropriate component drawing to illustrate them. Once you start
S (31) 001		Schedule of manholes	getting half-a-dozen types, however, and each type may vary as regards its head and jamb assembly, ironmongery and architrave, then it becomes a better bet to number the components on the plan and to refer the searcher to a schedule in which can be tabulated all the variables applying to a given component.

The three main schedules in this set are of this kind. Each gives a numbered list of manholes and openings and uses this as the starting point from which to refer to drawings covering all the variables affecting the component.

The ironmongery schedules are rather different in purpose and in format. They are essentially vocabularies of fittings, made up into sets. The opening schedules call up the set of fittings to be fixed to the relevant door or window.

*The examples given are sufficient to illustrate the principle. In practice, other component drawings might cover, for example: copings, pre-cast cladding panels (21), stairs, cat-ladders (24), lintels (31) and (32), balustrades (34), roof lights (37), skirtings (42), litter bins and bollards (70).

Peter Leach Associates	REGISTER OF **PRODUCTION** DRAWINGS					DRAWING CATEGORY	
PROJECT No.	TITLE					SHEET No.	
						TOTAL OF SHEETS IN CATEGORY	

Size	C1/Sfb	Number	Rev.	Description	Status	Remarks
	( )					
	( )					
	( )					
	( )					
	( )					
	( )					
	( )					
	( )					
	( )					
	( )					
	( )					
	( )					
	( )					
	( )					
	( )					
	( )					
	( )					
	( )					
	( )					
	( )					
	( )					
	( )					
	( )					
	( )					
	( )					
	( )					
	( )					
	( )					
	( )					
	( )					

CONTINUED ON SHEET No.

Columns Revision and Status are to be completed in pencil for up-dating.
The following codes are used;

1.	**Drawing Category**	2.	**Drawing Status**
L	= Location Drawing	E	= Detail Design Drawing
A	= Assembly Drawing	F	= Final Production Drawing
C	= Component Drawing	G	= Drawing Reconciled with B.Q.
S	= Sub-Component Drawing	K	= Construction Drawing
IN	= Information Drawing	M	= As Constructed Drawing

5.8   *A useful format for the drawing register. The explanatory notes help site staff as well as the drawing office*

It may not be released for construction, however, until it becomes:

K: *Construction drawing*. Finally, and where the need for record drawings justifies it, the drawing becomes:

M: *As constructed*.

This enables drawings to be issued for information only, without fear that, for example, the quantity surveyor will measure from an incomplete drawing or that the contractor will build from unauthorised information (**5.9**).

The method is also of value when a drawing is prepared as a basis for a manufacturer to prepare his own component drawing. In this case the architect prepares his own reference drawing with a status E. This is issued to the manufacturer, whose own working drawing is issued to site, the architect's drawing remaining at status E.

A typical drawing number, containing all the information referred to above, would be as shown in **5.10**.

CAD considerations

The addition of status coding is a useful adjunct to the issue of CAD files also, the status reference being added to the layer naming convention reference

THIS DRAWING WAS USED IN THE PREPARATION OF THE BILLS OF QUANTITIES.

ALL REVISIONS LISTED BELOW THIS LINE HAVE BEEN MADE SINCE THE BILLS OF QUANTITIES WERE PREPARED.

5.9 *Status coding of a drawing indicates only its status at the present time. This stamp freezes the drawing at the point when it relates to the other contract documents and is invaluable in managing the contract*

described later. However, CAD introduces additional requirements. CAD drawings are often plotted 'in house', with each plot requiring little more effort than a couple of mouse clicks. Very soon you have dozens of prints, each superseding the previous in some minor detail and possibly ten minutes apart. It is not practicable to provide each revision with a unique revision letter.

A practice might also be maintaining multiple copies of a drawing file on different computers, or in different sub-directories on the same computer; some may be back-up copies in case of hard disk failure; some may represent different stages in the evolution of the design. For internal purposes a practice will need to know more about a drawing plot than just its number and title.

One solution is to have a second 'For Office Use Only' identifying code printed elsewhere on the drawing, including the time and date the plot is made plus the full file name and computer path of the originating CAD file. If placed in the opposite corner of the print and outside the margins of the drawing proper, confusion with the 'public' title panel should be avoided. In this way the version of a plotted version can always be identified (**5.11**). (As a bonus, this information can also be written to a simple text file, providing a crude record of drawings plotted.)

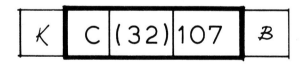

5.10 *A full drawing number, using the system described. The number within the heavy box is the drawing's unique identification and is the minimum information required by anyone searching for it.*
It indicates that the drawing is of a component filling an internal opening and that it is number 107 in the series. The K at the left indicates that the drawing has been released for constructional purposes. The issue is Revision B

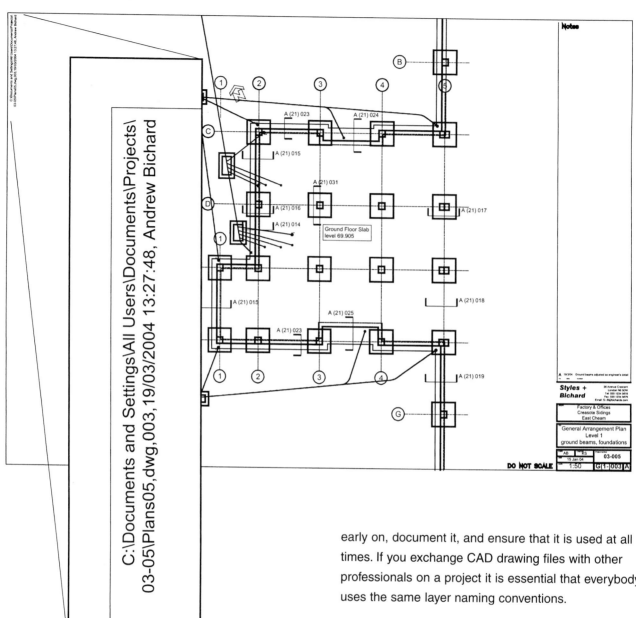

C:\Documents and Settings\All Users\Documents\Projects\
03-05\Plans05,dwg,003,19/03/2004 13:27:48, Andrew Bichard

5.11 *Coding system for internal office use*

Similarly, an efficient and properly documented layer naming convention is essential. It is no good drawing something on a layer and then forgetting where it is. You need to establish a naming convention for your practice

early on, document it, and ensure that it is used at all times. If you exchange CAD drawing files with other professionals on a project it is essential that everybody uses the same layer naming conventions.

Proper naming of layers within the model is important to ensure that each professional can establish 'ownership' of the layers that they create. The Layer Naming Standard set out in BS 1192 Part 5 makes provision for including an ownership code within each layer name. Depending on the CAD program used it may even be possible for each professional to lock their layers with password protection, preventing other members of the design team editing them (intentionally or otherwise) without their consent.

Portable document format

Portable document format (PDF) has long been a *de facto* standard for the distribution and exchange of electronic documents. It is a computer file format that preserves the fonts, images, graphics and layout of any source document, regardless of the application and platform used to create it. Adobe © PDF can be viewed and printed by anyone with free Adobe © software which can be sent along with the file, or downloaded from the Internet.

Unlike their originating source files created with CAD or word processing programs, PDF files cannot be edited. They are therefore of no use when a two-way exchange of information is needed. But where it is necessary to provide information in a secure and reliable electronic form that can be viewed or printed by the recipient, yet cannot be modified, they are ideal. From version 6 onwards, PDF files have supported layers that can be turned on or off by the recipient, giving them more flexibility when viewing or printing CAD documents.

The major CAD programs have built in ability to create either PDF files, or an equivalent such as AutoCAD's DWF.

Simple PDF creation programs can be downloaded from the internet free of charge.

Circulation

The greater the use that is made of the drawing register the more important does it become to exercise proper discipline in its maintenance and circulation. In particular, it is a useful procedure for the up-dated register (and those of the other consultants) to be copied to all concerned at regular intervals—e.g. on the first of each month, or as part of the site meeting agenda—so that all team members are aware of the up-to-date position. This is of even greater importance when drawings are being issued in sequence, whether for billing or construction purposes. The recipient's attitude to a given drawing will

be conditioned by his knowledge that further amplifying details are envisaged as part of the complete set.

Other people's drawings

When other consultants are circulating CAD files their receipt should be registered and filed under the recipient's own file storage system.

The proper recording and storage of incoming drawings however often presents a problem, particularly when their numbering system bears no relation to the structure of the architect's set. Should one open up an incoming drawings' register for each consultant and manufacturer, laboriously entering drawing titles and number and date of receipt? Should one even attempt to give each incoming drawing a fresh number, to bring it into line with internal systems, and to aid storage and subsequent retrieval?

These methods are laborious and irksome, and unless they are carried through 100 per cent efficiently they are liable to break down. If only one drawing goes unrecorded because it was needed urgently for reference purposes at the workplace before anyone had time to enter it in the register, the system collapses, and might as well have never been started.

It is far better to insist on all consultants preparing and circulating their own drawing register in the way previously described. Each office then has a document against which incoming issues may be checked, and by means of which possible omissions and out-of-date revisions may be noted.

As for the storage of incoming drawings, they may be dealt with in the same way as one's own prints and negatives, and stored in drawers or hung vertically. Alternatively, they may be folded into A4 size with the drawing number outermost, and stored upright on shelves in numerical order. This is simple and space-saving, but presupposes that a drawing register is available in which the search for the required drawing may be initiated.

Issuing drawings

It has already been noted that the drawing register is not a convenient document for recording the issue of drawings to others, neither, although it is sometimes used for this purpose, is the drawing itself. Indeed, one should first start by questioning the need for such a record in the first place. That drawings, both on completion and on subsequent revision, should go to the people who need them, is perhaps self-evident. Yet instances abound of site staff working from out-of-date information, of revision B going to the structural engineer but not the M & E consultant, of the quantity surveyor being unaware of the expensive revised detail agreed on site and hastily confirmed by a sketch to the contractor but not to him. The fundamental question for anyone engaged in preparing working drawings—who am I doing this for?—needs to be asked yet again here. Whoever it is being drawn for needs it, and the common-sense procedure of mentally running through the list of everybody whose understanding of the job is remotely changed by the preparation of the new drawing or revision is a valuable discipline for reducing communication gaps. Send to too many rather than to too few is a good maxim.

The keeping of a drawings issue register, however, will not of itself guarantee that the right people get the right drawings. The best we can achieve is to set up disciplines which, if they cannot prevent errors and omissions, can at least assist their detection in due time.

Two such disciplines may be mentioned. First, the use of a drawings issue slip when any drawing leaves the office—even though accompanied by a covering letter—provides an easily leafed-through file record in the issuing drawing office (**5.12**). Second, the routine issue at regular intervals to all members of the team—contractors, sub-contractors and consultants alike—of the drawing register. This at least enables the recipient to check that they are working to the latest revision of a given drawing, and to some extent throws the onus on them for ensuring that their information is up to date.

As to the more mundane question of physically conveying a package of drawings from one office to another, then the larger drawings, unless they are rolled (which is irritating for the recipient) will be folded down to A4 or A3, depending on their volume, and always, of course, with the title panel on the outside (see **4.19** and **4.20**).

Small drawings, whether of A4 or A3 format, should not be issued loose when they form a set. Their use is sometimes criticised, especially by builders, but a lot of this criticism stems from their misuse in practice rather than from any inherent defect in their size. They are only difficult to coordinate if no logical search pattern holds the set together, and they only get out of sequence or get lost if they are issued unbound. It is important therefore that sets of small drawings should be treated as instruction manuals rather than individual sheets, and should be held together accordingly in simple folders (loose-leaf to facilitate photocopying for issue to suppliers by the contractor). It is anomalous that the motor engineer assembling a car in the protected conditions of a factory or workshop should be given a book of instructions to work from, while the building operative working on precarious scaffolding and battling against wind and rain should traditionally be expected to work from loose sheets of paper flapping round him.

It is appropriate that such bound manuals should contain the drawing register, and some form of guide to the drawing method.

One approach with CAD is to publish *all* drawings in electronic format on a secure 'members only' website. All the team can see the latest revisions and can call for their own copy if needed. This puts the onus on recipients to request drawings rather than on the architect to issue them.

TO:- Mr Gray Peter Leach Associates	FROM:-	**CLARK & FENN LTD** **MITCHAM HOUSE** **681 MITCHAM ROAD** **CROYDON, CR9 3AP** **01-689 2288**

TITLE OF CONTRACT *Leeds Permanent Building Society, Epsom*

JOB No. Z 7375

Please find herewith for:-

‡ (Please put tick in appropriate box)

☐ **APPROVAL**

☑ **RECORDS**

☐ **DISTRIBUTION**

drawings as listed below

DRG NO	REVISION LETTER	TITLE	NO OF COPIES
A2809/1		*Ceiling Layout + Details*	2

Signed for Clark & Fenn Ltd. *G Allbright*

Date *7·8·81*

TO RECIPIENT:-

Please sign and return duplicate copy

These drawings are

as ‡

☐ **APPROVED** — — — copies requ'd for distribution

☐ **APPROVED SUBJECT TO COMMENTS NOTED**

☐ **RETURNED FOR AMENDMENT & RE-SUBMISSION**

Signed _____

Date _____

5.12 *Drawing issues form accompanying all drawings issued provides a convenient file record of such issues*

Drawings guide

It is no use preparing your drawings on a well structured and carefully thought out basis if you are the only one who knows about it. Until such time as a standard drawing method becomes universally employed and recognised throughout the building industry—and despite the increasing emphasis being laid on the Coordinated Project Information documents previously referred to we are still a long way from that—it is incumbent on the producing office to give clear directions as to how its drawings may best be used.

Instruction must take two forms if it is to be effective. There must be a verbal explanation of the method, when the building team is shown the search pattern for information. The initial site meeting is a useful venue for this. There must also be a written guide for subsequent reference, and this will be a useful document to bind into the office manual. Newcomers to the office need to know how the office method works.

An office manual which embodies the drawing and coding methods advocated in this handbook could be prepared for use by other members of the office, other consultants and contractors alike. It might be set out as shown below.

A Guide to these Drawings

The drawings in this project have been arranged in the following manner:

1.0) All information in the drawing set is divided into five basic categories of drawing. These are (relating for example to windows):

- General arrangement drawing (coded G) showing **where** anything is—e.g. where a particular window is located in the building. (This includes general arrangement plans and elevations, locating all major building elements— walls, doors, windows, etc.—and indicating where more detailed information may be found.

- Component drawing (coded C) showing **what** it is— e.g. what the window looks like, how big it is, etc. (This includes the size and appearance of all components—windows, doors, shutters, fitments, cupboards, etc.).

- Assembly drawing (coded A) showing **how** it is incorporated in the building—e.g. how the window relates to the sill and to the wall in which it is built. (Demonstrating the manner in which the various building elements and components fit together. Storey sections through external walls are an obvious instance.)

- Sub-component drawing (coded SC) showing the detailed construction of each component—e.g. the section of the window frame. (A timber window, for example, would be treated as a component— coded C—whereas sections of its frame, glazing, beads, etc. would be the subject of an SC drawing.)

- Schedule (coded S), providing an index to the retrieval of information from other sources, and tabulating items—e.g. windows, doors, manholes, etc.—located on other drawings throughout the building.

- Information drawing (coded IN) giving supplementary information which is relevant, but not part of the building—e.g. survey drawings, bore hole analyses, etc.

2.0) Each category is then divided into broad sections or elements, each of which deals with a different subject. The codes for these are given in brackets following the drawing category, as follows:

(1-) Substructure.

(2-) Primary elements
(i.e. walls, floors, roofs, stairs, frames).

(3-) Secondary elements
(i.e. everything filling openings in walls, floors and roofs; suspended ceilings and balustrades).

(4-) Finishes.

(5-) Services.

(6-) Installations.

(7-) Fixtures
(i.e. sanitary fittings, cupboards, shelving, etc.).

(8-) Loose equipment (i.e. fire extinguishers, unfixed furniture, etc.).

(—) The project in general
(i.e. information of a general nature which cannot readily be allocated to any of the preceding elements).

3.0) All of these codes will not necessarily be used on any one project. A list of the elements into which the present set is divided is given at the end of this guide. The element will always be recognisable from the drawing number box however. For example:

G(2-)003 is a general arrangement drawing, and deals with the positioning and referencing of primary elements. It is the third drawing in that series.

C(3-)012 is a component drawing, and is of a secondary element component, such as a door or a roof light. It is the twelfth drawing in that series.

4.0) One further sub-division is built into the system. (C3-) indicates that the drawing deals with a secondary element component. (C32) however indicates that it is a secondary component in an internal wall, and (C37) that it is a secondary element in a roof. A complete table (known as CI/SfB Table I) is given below. Once again all these sub-divisions will not necessarily appear in this drawing set. Furthermore you may well find a general arrangement drawing coded GA(3-) covering all secondary elements but containing in it references to component drawings (C31), (C32), C(37), etc. This is so that component drawings relating to windows, internal doors and roof lights, respectively, may be grouped together for easy reference.

As noted above, the complete CI/SfB Table 1 should be included. (If, of course, the Uniclass coding system is being used then a complete copy of Uniclass Table G should be provided, and the individual element references should be to that system.)

Other consultants' drawings

Little has been said so far about the drawings of other consultants and it may be appropriate to comment here on the problems of liaison and coordination of drawings produced outside the architect's immediate control. Part of the difficulty arises from the fact that neither the structural engineer nor his M & E counterpart really produces production drawings in the strict sense of the term as it has been used here, i.e. as a definitive instruction to the builder. Each produces traditionally what is in effect a design drawing, relying on others to provide supplementary information for construction purposes. For example, the structural engineer constantly relies on the architect's drawings to convey such fundamental information as chases in upstand beams for asphalt, throatings in soffits and the required finish for exposed in situ concrete. The M & E consultant is more often than not unable to provide information on, for example, holding down bolts because the position of these is dependent upon a plant manufacturer who may not have been selected at the time he considered his drawing effort complete. So 'See architect's detail' appears on the structural drawing (if we are lucky) and 'See manufacturer's shop drawing for setting out of pockets' is frequently the best that can be achieved by M & E. Neither is very satisfactory, yet the difficulties in effecting an improvement are substantial, for both spring from a historical and artificial fragmentation of the building process: in the first instance a fragmentation of professional disciplines; in the second an unnatural alienation of the designer and the constructor.

Changing roles

Changing the roles of the profession and the industry may well be desirable, but it is a long-term process and not the function of this book. The best must be made of the present situation. It is therefore incumbent on the architect to acknowledge his management function as coordinator of the professional team, and he must accept responsibility for ensuring that the structural engineer is aware of M & E requirements, and that M & E are equally aware of structural constraints. In an imperfect world nobody else is going to do this.

Elemental drawings

Another consideration must be that if we are dealing, as proposed, with a largely elementalised set of drawings as an aid to communication between designer and operative, then it ought to be made possible for a carpenter to build his formwork from the engineer's drawings alone, without the need to refer to drawings prepared by others for information which may be vital to him.

Requirement of a formal meeting

It is beneficial for drawings which are to be prepared by others to be agreed at a formal meeting, which can be minuted. Clearly the architect is in a better position if he has firm proposals and methods worked out to put to the meeting than if he throws the meeting open to suggestions from all sides.

Design team meeting

Such a meeting should cover the following points:

1   *Introductions*. Individuals in each organisation must be named as the link men through whom information is to be channelled. They should be of sufficient standing to be able to act and make decisions responsibly and with authority and, if possible, they should be of comparable standing within their own organisations. It is unhelpful to the project for a

young project architect to be out-gunned by the senior partner of the engineering consultants.

2 *Procedures*. The means by which all team members are to be kept informed must be established. There is no necessity for the architect to insist on acting as a post office, nor need he insist on being party to day-to-day discussions between other consultants, but it is vital that he be kept informed of the outcome of such discussions and that all drawing exchanges are copied to him.

3 *Programme*. An example of a programme for the design team has been given in **5.6**. Table it, but do not insist unreasonably on its detailed initial acceptance by other team members against their better judgement. It must at all costs be realistic. But once it has been accepted, it must be taken seriously. Tongue-in-cheek agreement with one eye on an escape route when the inevitable problems occur can be a costly business for everyone.

4 *Format*. Thought should have been given at the design stage of the project to the question of suitable production drawing scales and sizes, so the architect should be well prepared to table his proposals for the format. Consistency between all drawing producing offices is important. Apart from the demonstrable advantages of enabling the architect's basic drawings to be used by other consultants and the reduction of storage and retrieval problems on site, the indefinable authority generated by a well-organised set of drawings and the impression given of a team well in control of affairs all help in promoting confidence in the team among both outsiders and its own members.

Note that the desirability of maintaining a consistent format applies equally to computer-aided drawings. With the possible exception of drawings transmitted electronically—model exchange, for example—communication between offices will be by means of drawings in the form of hard copies on paper.

5 *Coding of drawings*. If the model exchange method for producing CAD information is in operation, it is a

sine qua non that all professional offices involved in the project will be using it. With this exception it is not essential for all consultants to follow the structuring and coding disciples that the architect imposes on himself. Nevertheless, it is highly desirable that they should be persuaded to do so. In practice it should not be very onerous. All disciplines have their equivalent of the general arrangement drawing, and all use schedules. These are worth bringing into the structuring method, even though the structural engineer may still adopt his traditional practice of inserting larger scale sections on his general arrangement drawings. If CI/SfB is in use then blanket codes of (16) Foundations and (28) Frame for structural drawings and of (5-) Services and (6-) Installations for services engineers' drawings provide a simple expedient for bringing all disciplines within a common retrieval framework without launching others on to waters, the depth of which the architect may not yet have plumbed fully.

It is important that layer naming for CAD should be agreed in advance by all the professional team.

6 *Definition of responsibilities*. Many defects, both of omission and of overlapping information, may be avoided if the responsibilities of each team member can be defined precisely at the outset of the project. Apart from the more straightforward contractual responsibilities which it is assumed will have been covered in the respective letters of appointment but which it will be sensible to confirm at this inaugural meeting (matters such as, for example, who tackles lifts, cold water supply, drainage, roads and footpaths; who details and checks pre-cast concrete components, etc.)—these are grey areas where some early agreement will be of benefit. The allocation to the structural drawing office of the responsibility for indicating accurately detailed profiles has already been referred to. Reinforced concrete staircases provide another area where it is unnecessary and confusing for the architect to prepare elaborately detailed sections for the benefit

of a contractor who is going to build from the structural engineer's drawings anyway. An early agreement should be reached to limit the architect's role to providing design profiles within which the structural engineer may work, and against which the structural details may be subsequently checked.

Drawing office programming

The design team programme will have identified the time available for production of the working drawings, and the first shot at the drawing register will have revealed the magnitude of the task. The reconciliation of one with the other, and of both with the financial resources available, is one of the essential arts of architectural management and as such demands more space than can be devoted to it in this handbook. Certain points may usefully be made however.

Size of drawing office team

The right size and structure of the team is all-important, and in many ways it is a case of the smaller the better. Any increase over a team of one starts to invoke the law of diminishing returns and as the numbers increase so do the problems of control and communications. On the other hand, the diversity of work demanded by most building projects coupled with the constant and remorseless pressures of the overall programme mean that too small a team lacks the necessary flexibility of response.

In practical terms, the size of the team will be the size of the tasks in man-weeks divided by the number of weeks available, and if the latter is unreasonably low then the team becomes unwieldy and difficult to coordinate. In any case, the size of the team is bound to fluctuate throughout the working drawing period, with a small but high-powered element at stage E, rising to a peak soon after commencement of stage F, and tailing off towards the end of that stage as the main flow of information to the quantity surveyor is completed **5.13**.

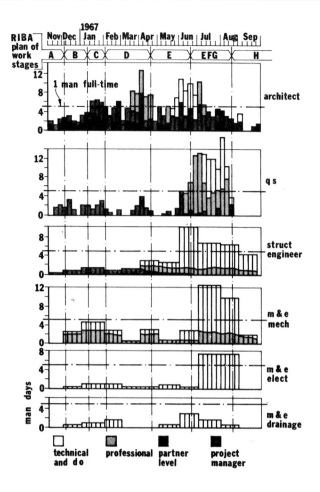

5.13 *This histogram, taken from the records of an actual project, shows the difficulties of coordinating multi-disciplinary efforts. The peaking of resources during the production drawing stage is clearly shown*

When the office is working with CAD it is probable that for more than one drawing position will be linked to the printer/plotter, which may well be inoperative for long periods. Unless the team is very small and its members are in constant touch with one another it is essential to have some form of unified control so that the printer/plotter is not operated from two drawing positions simultaneously (or that everyone has a small printer/plotter for check plots).

Backing up is also essential. Data are the most valuable thing you own; guard them well. With manual drawings your data are stored as negatives and prints and carbon copies of letters in filing cabinets. If they were destroyed by fire it would be possible to recover most of the lost information by getting copies back from the client, colleagues, contractor, and so on. Possibly you had backed-up to microfiche, and kept copies away from the office.

With CAD everything is kept on disk. All your data are concentrated in one place, the hard disk. This is very efficient, but it does allow the possibility of losing everything at once. No technology is perfect and can and will fail eventually, often without warning. Full and frequent back-up procedures are essential. Back-ups should be kept away from the office, in a fire-proof safe, or preferably both. All back-up media have a limited life.

Production drawing programme

The production drawings, if properly structured so that a predetermined amount of information is conveyed in them, should be the simplest aspect of the architect's work to quantify in terms of time taken. Having established the list of drawings, it is better for two of the more experienced people to make independent assessments of the time that should be taken over each drawing and to compare notes afterwards. Factors of personal optimism or pessimism may thus be discounted, and a more realistic time allocation made. But experience is everything, and an inquest after the programme has been completed, with feedback of the actual time taken over each drawing as against the time budgeted for, is essential if future programmes are to be timed more accurately.

Priorities

In framing the stage F programme certain priorities will emerge. Clearly, the establishment of the basic set of general arrangement plans is fundamental, for they will form the basis for elementalisation of subsequent general arrangement plans and of other consultants' work. After that the priorities will probably be dictated by the needs of the quantity surveyor. An elemental format makes it easier to group the issue of drawings into separate packages—e.g. internal joinery, finishes, etc., but this is only helpful if the packages are genuinely complete. Few quantity surveyors will object to receiving information piecemeal, but an early issue of the openings schedule with half the details it refers to still incomplete, only leads to an abortive start being made on the measurement. On the other hand, the fact that drawings of the basic structure may be issued and measured without having to wait for the finishes to be added to the same sheet does allow a bigger overlap of the production drawings and billing programmes.

Drawings should be allocated to team members in the form of a simple bar chart. By this means, everyone can see his personal short-term and long-term targets (**5.14**).

Introducing new methods

When *Working Drawings Handbook* first appeared in 1982 the concept of structured drawings was alien to many drawing offices. Their number has now diminished, but the following notes are intended for offices which have still not taken the plunge.

The introduction of structured drawings into an office which hitherto has managed without them requires some thought. There must be many offices which, whilst agreeing in principle that their work could be improved by rationalisation of their working drawing methods, are reluctant to take the first step on what might prove to be a seductively attractive slippery slope.

As with dieting and exercise, the two important things are to start today rather than tomorrow and not to be put off by the prophecies of failure which will be made by those around you. In this latter respect, one common fallacy may be dispelled at the outset. You will be told

142

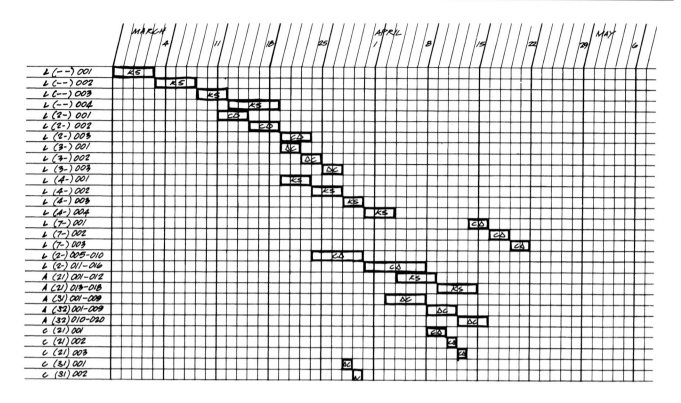

5.14 *A drawing office programme allocates individual team members appropriate work loads. The elemental approach means that DC, for example, can follow the (3-) element right through, dealing with it in its general arrangement, component and assembly aspects*

confidently that architects are individualists and will fight tooth and nail against any suggestion of rationalised drawing, standardised detailing or mathematically oriented coding systems. This you will find to be untrue, architects being as fundamentally lazy and anxious for a trouble-free existence as anyone else. Experience indicates that given a common-sense system which is fundamentally easy to use, people will use it.

The sequence to take

However, take one step at a time. There are several degrees of rationalisation and they should be introduced in sequence:

- Standardise drawing size and format for all new projects entering production drawing stage.

- Rationalise new projects into the general arrangement, assembly, component, sub-component, schedule format.

- Select one such project for the experimental application of CI/SfB (or Uniclass) coding and let it run through its production phase before attempting a general application of the method. You will thus have built up some office case law to assist in answering the query 'How do we code for this situation?' which will arise on subsequent projects.

- Now that you have each project producing component and assembly information in a common format and within the context of a coding system offering ease of retrieval, you are in a position, if you so wish, to introduce standard solutions to various aspects of your detailing.

What does it cost?

As to the cost of introducing (and indeed of operating) new drawing methods one is on less certain ground. Certainly all the available feedback suggests that it is unusual for a practice to revert to unstructured working drawings once it has started producing structured sets, which seems to indicate that at least the structured set is not so overwhelmingly expensive to produce as to render it uneconomic in practice. Short of carrying out parallel drawing exercises using two methods and comparing the cost there is no real way of being sure.

What is clear, however, is that the more comprehensive nature of the information likely to be produced within a structured format, its greater potential for coordination, and the greater ease of information retrieval which it offers to the contractor, will all combine to reduce time-consuming queries once the work is on site. An honest analysis of office time spent on so-called 'site operations' is perhaps a salutary exercise for any practice. Bearing in mind that the plan of work defines stage K as consisting of 'Administration of the building contract up to and including practical completion. Provision to the contractor of further information as and when reasonably required', consider how much time in practice is spent in the drawing office in amending existing drawings and in providing new ones to illustrate details which could (and in retrospect clearly should) have been provided during the working drawings stage. Consider also the predictable reaction of the poor unfortunate who is dragged back a year later from the multi-million pounds fantasy on which he is happily engaged in order to sort out the door detail he had unfortunately omitted from the working drawing set which had been his previous task. It must always be cheaper to produce information at the right time.

On the other hand, any change in working method must have some cost implication, as the change to metric dimensioning demonstrated. As with metrication, this cost should be looked upon as an investment for the future.

And the future?

A whole new world of technology lies ahead of us. But it is difficult to visualise a bricklayer laying bricks other than by using a paper drawing to instruct him where to lay them. The role of the architect and of the architectural drawing office appear to be secure for the foreseeable future.

The more important consideration is: how will CAD itself develop?

The twenty-first century looks like being an exciting one.

APPENDIX 1

Building elements and external features

The degree of detail used in representing any element is dependent on the scale at which it is shown. The examples given below give an indication of what may be considered appropriate for various scales.

Windows

Scale 1:200

Scale 1:100

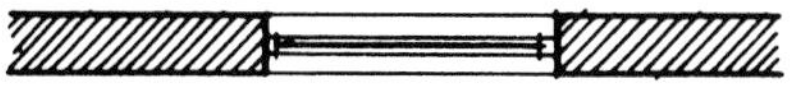

Scale 1:50
and over

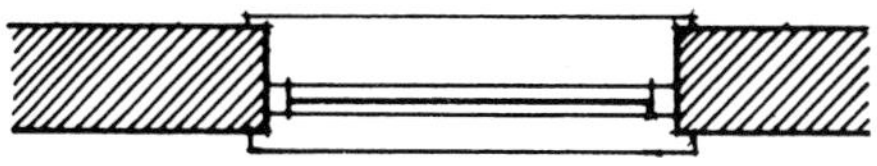

Doors

Scale 1:200

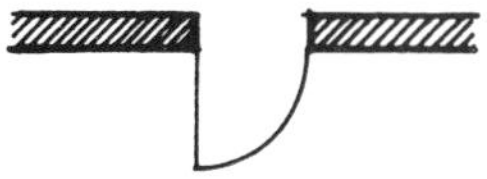

Scale 1:100

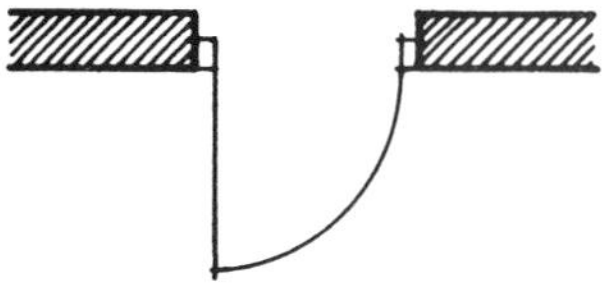

Scale 1:50
and over

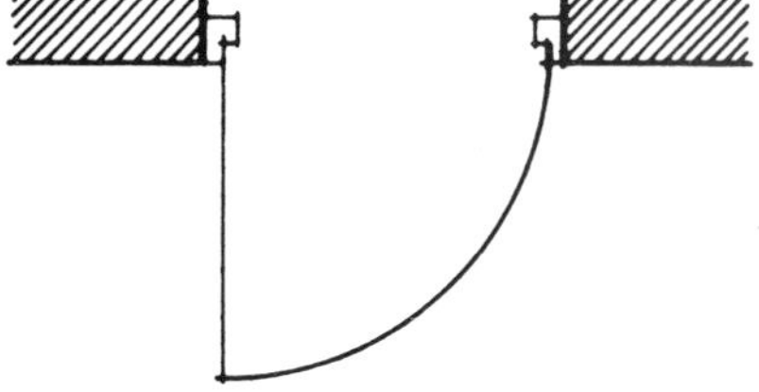

Manholes

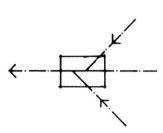

Scale 1 : 100 and under

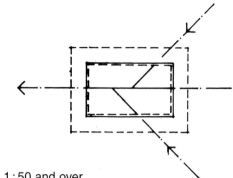

Scale 1 : 50 and over

Staircases

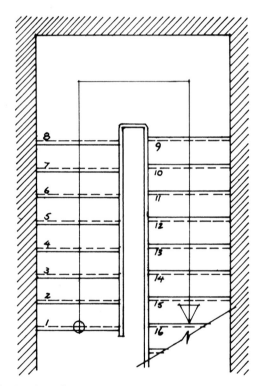

Scale 1 : 50 and over

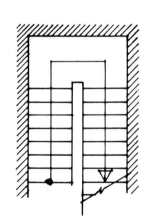

Scale 1 : 100 and under

External features

Contours (existing)

15·000

Contours (proposed)

15·000

Grading (the arrows point to the lowest level)

Woodland (existing)

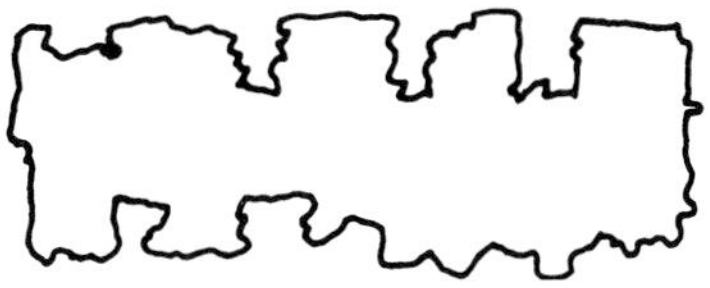

Woodland (proposed)

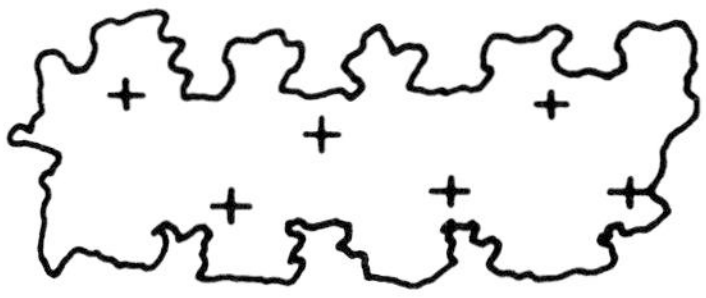

Trees: 1 existing
2 to be removed
3 new

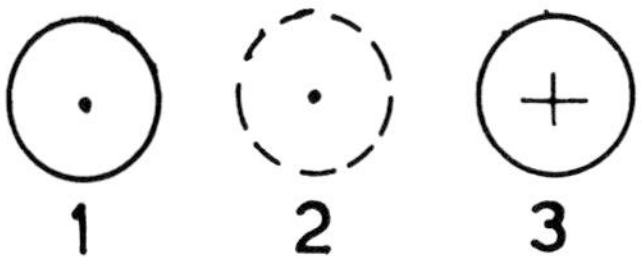

1   2   3

Hedge (existing)

Hedge (proposed)

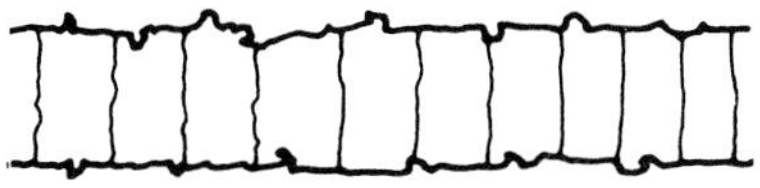

Grass

Fence

Features in fence:
1 gate
2 stile

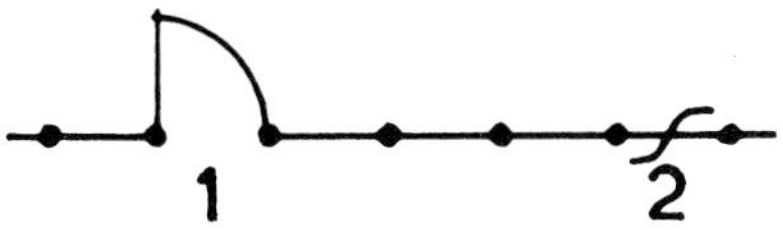

1   2

Conventions for doors and windows

Doors

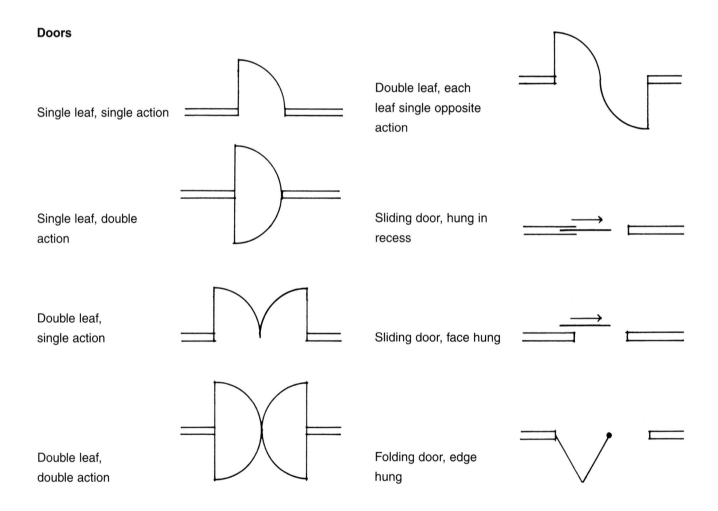

Single leaf, single action

Single leaf, double action

Double leaf, single action

Double leaf, double action

Double leaf, each leaf single opposite action

Sliding door, hung in recess

Sliding door, face hung

Folding door, edge hung

148

Folding door, centre hung

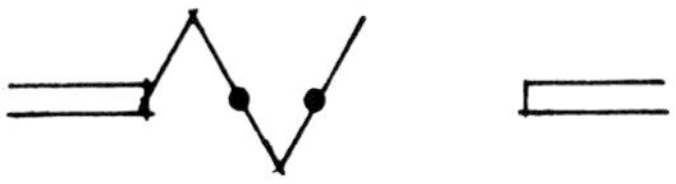

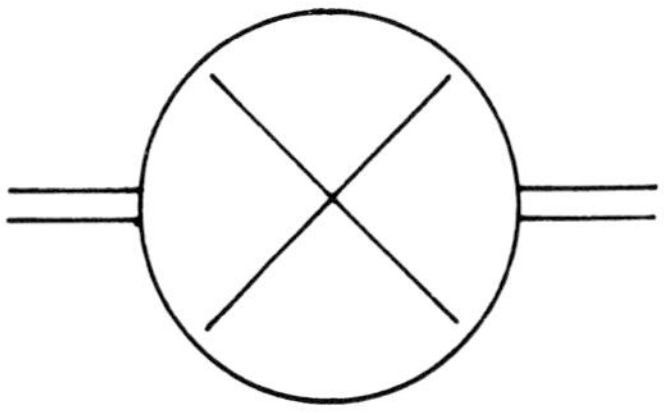

Revolving door

Windows

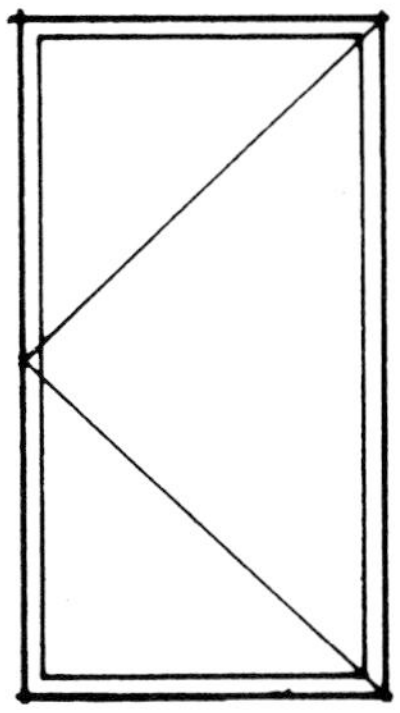

Side hung casement (L.H.)

Top hung casement (opening out unless otherwise stated)

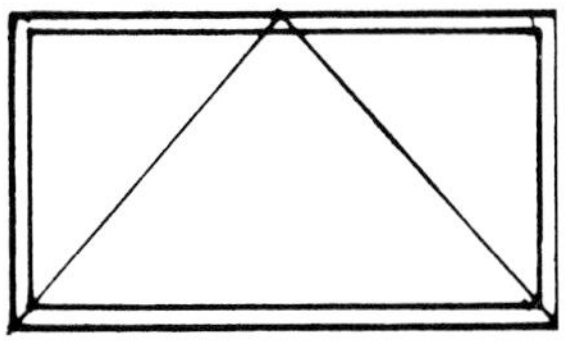

Bottom hung hopper (opening in unless otherwise stated)

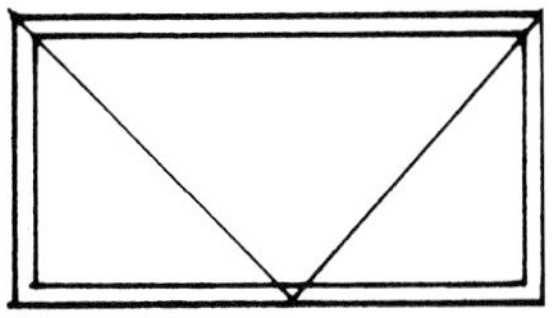

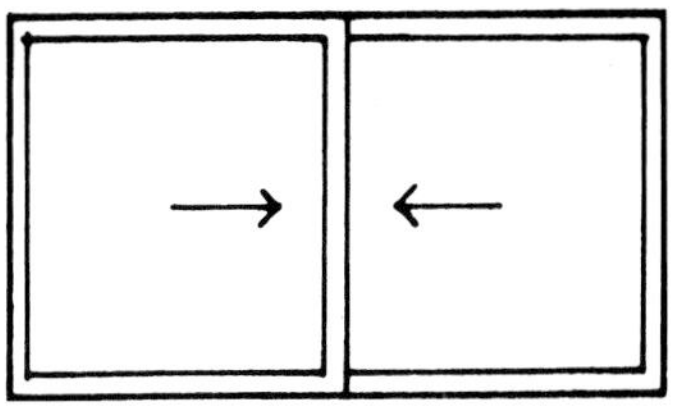

Horizontal sliding sash

Vertical pivot (opening edge should be stated)

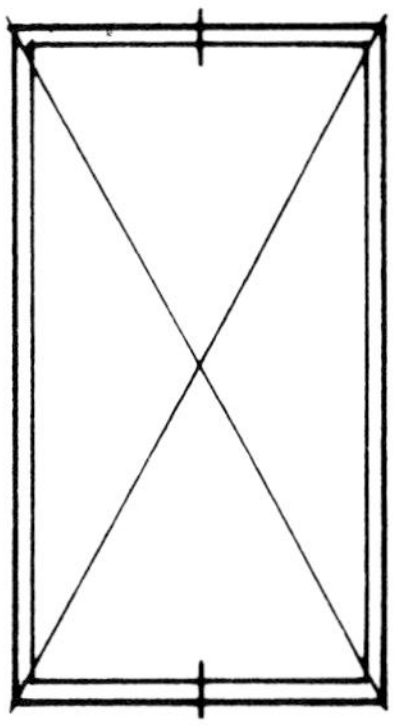

Horizontal pivot (bottom edge opens out unless otherwise stated)

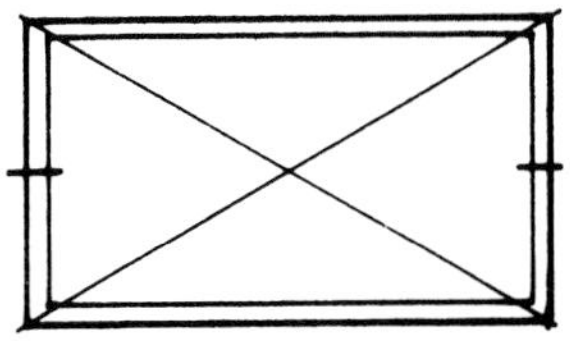

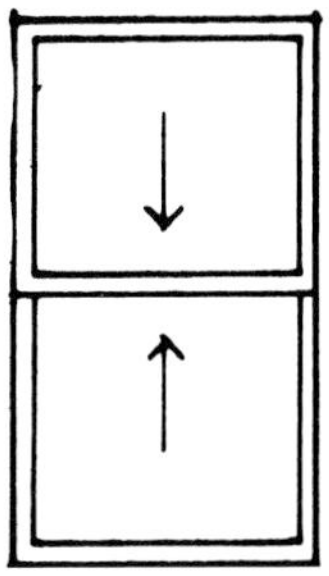

Vertical sliding sash

Convention assumes all windows are viewed from the outside

Symbols indicating materials

Blockwork

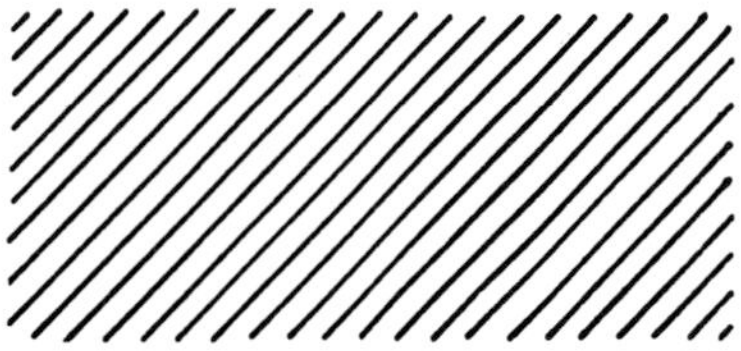

Hardcore

Brickwork

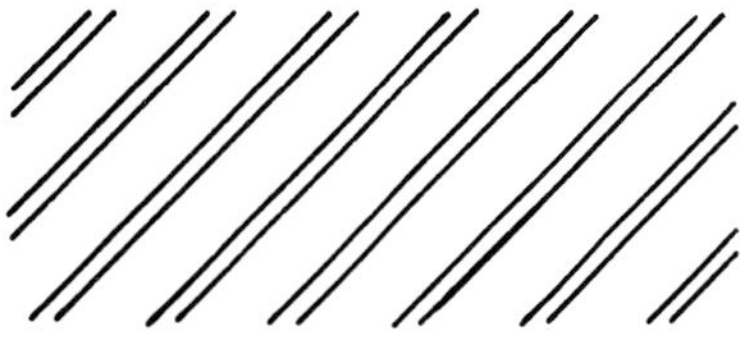

Precast concrete

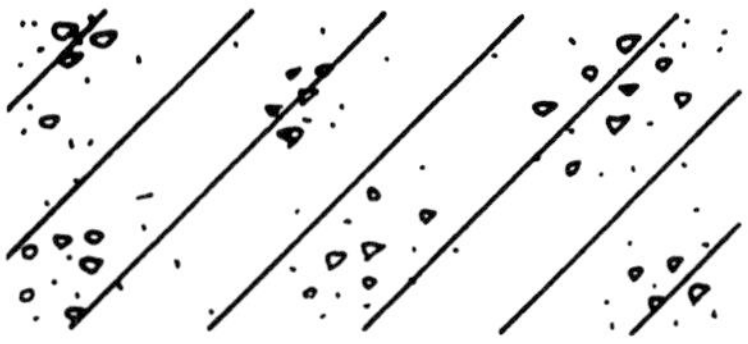

Earth

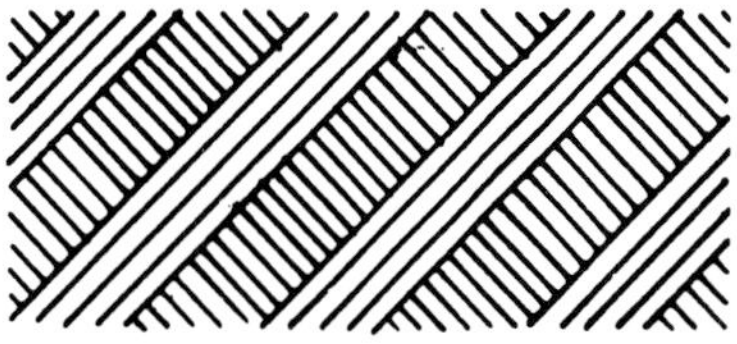

Blockwork
(commonly
used alternative)

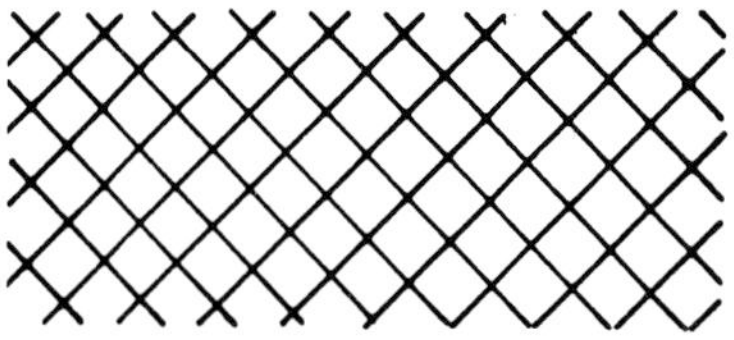

Concrete

Stone

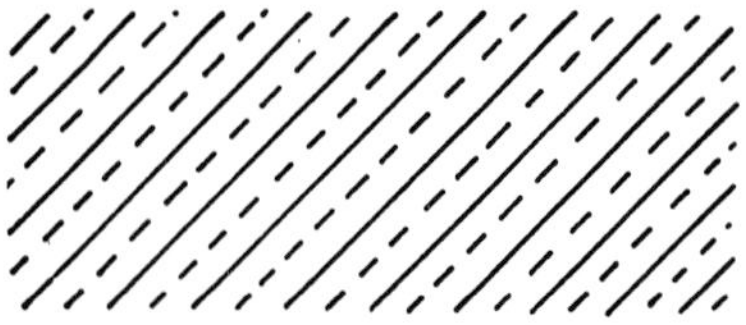

Marble

Rubble stonework

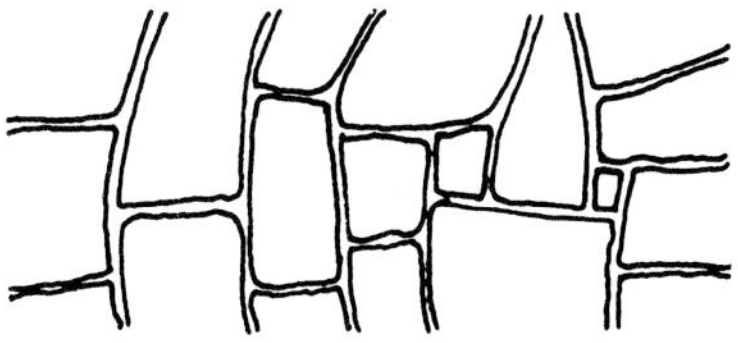

Slate

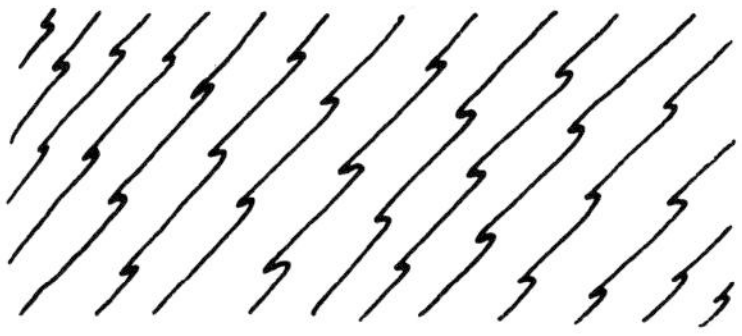

Insulation

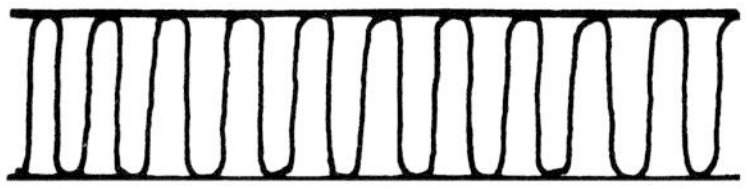

Unwrot timber section

Wrot timber section

Wrot timber section on two faces

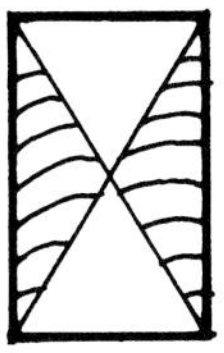

Metal (at large scale)

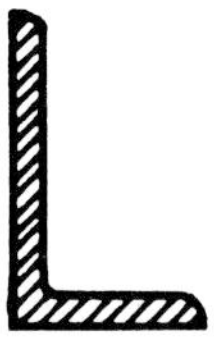

Metal (at small scale)

Plaster (or cement screed)

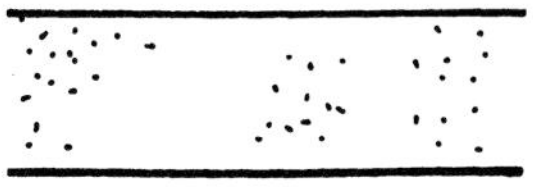

Some abbreviations in common use

alum.	aluminium
asb.	asbestos
bit.	bitumen (or bituminous)
bk.	brick
bkwk.	brickwork
C.I.	cast iron
conc.	concrete
cp.	chromium plated
h/wd.	hardwood
PVA.	polyvinyl acetate
PVC.	polyvinyl chloride
PCC.	pre-cast concrete
rfmt.	reinforcement
SAA.	satin anodised aluminium
SS.	stainless steel
s/wd.	softwood
t & g	tongued and grooved
UPVC.	unplasticised polyvinyl chloride
W.I.	wrought iron

Electrical, telecommunications and fire protection symbols

Extracts from British Standards Nos BS 1192 (1984–2000); BS 3939 (1986–1991) and BS 1635 (1990) are reproduced here with the permission of BSI under license number 2004DH0029. British Standards can be obtained from BSI Customer Services, 389 Chiswick High Road, London W4 4AL, Tel +44 (0)20 8996 9001, email: cservices@bsi-global.com

The symbols for use in these fields are covered in a number of publications, primarily:

BS 1192: 1984–2000 *Construction drawing practice (Pts I and II)*

BS3939: 1986–1991 *Graphical symbols for electrical power, telecommunications and electrics diagrams*

BS 1635: 1990 *Graphical symbols and abbreviations for fire protection drawings*

The symbols shown represent a small selection of those available. They have been restricted to those which the architect is most likely to encounter when dealing with the type of small-scale work in which an electrical consultant has not been appointed.

Certain symbols are differently represented in different Standards. Furthermore, other symbols have acquired a use in practice but do not appear in any laid down Standard. In such cases the most common usage has been given.

Reference should be made to the British Standards listed above for more comprehensive lists of symbols.

Main control or intake

Distribution board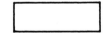

Earth

Consumer's earthing terminal

Single pole one way switch

Similar, but the number indicates the number of switches at one point

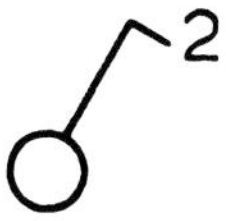

Key operated switch

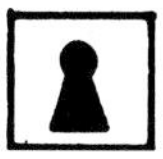

Two pole one way switch

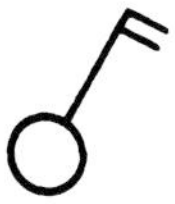

Socket outlet

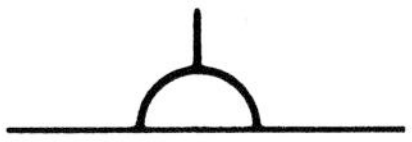

Cord operated single pole one way switch

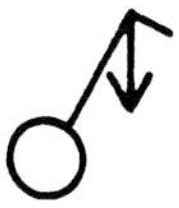

Switched socket outlet

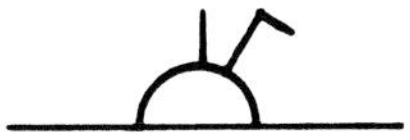

Two way switch

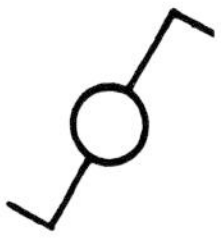

Double socket outlet

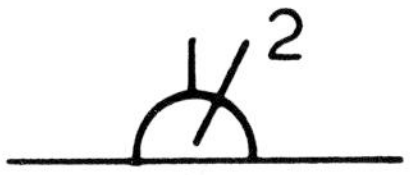

Dimmer switch

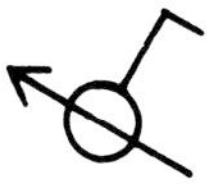

Lighting point—ceiling mounted

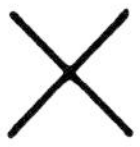

Period limiting switch

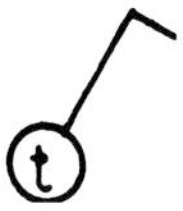

Emergency lighting point

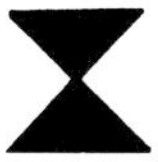

Time switch

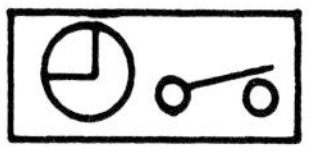

Lighting point—wall mounted

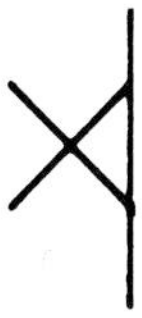

Thermostat

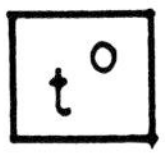

Lighting point with integral switch

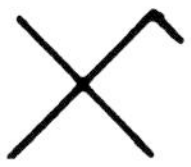

Push button

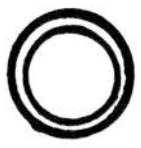

Single fluorescent lamp

Luminous push button

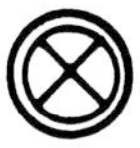

Three fluorescent lamps

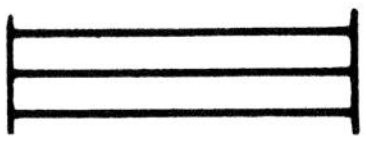

Outdoor lighting standard	Telephone point (internal only)
Outdoor lighting bollard	Public telephone point
Illuminated sign	Automatic telephone exchange equipment
Illuminated emergency sign	Automatic telex exchange equipment
Electric bell	Manual switchboard
Clock (or slave clock)	**Fire protection**
Master clock	Hydrant point

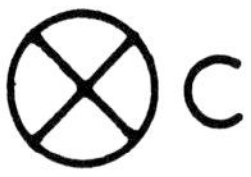

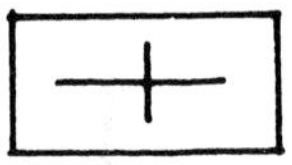

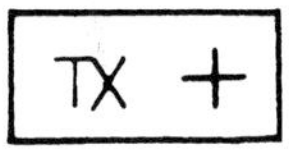

Telecommunications

Telecommunications socket outlet. State use—e.g. TV (for television) R (for radio), etc.

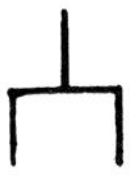

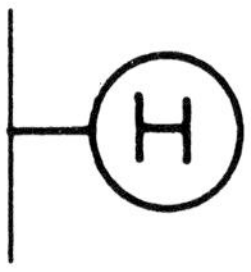

Wall valve—wet

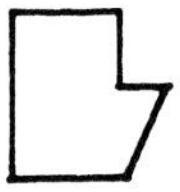

Wall valve—dry

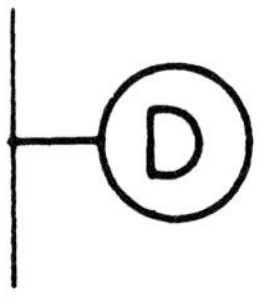

Aerial

Telephone point (to exchange lines) — Hose reel

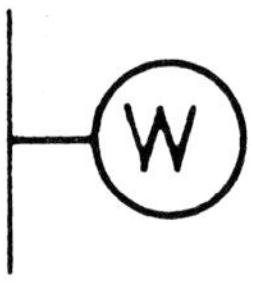

Fire extinguishers. Indicate type,
e.g. SA Soda Acid
    W   Water
    F   Foam
    CO_2 Carbon dioxide, etc.

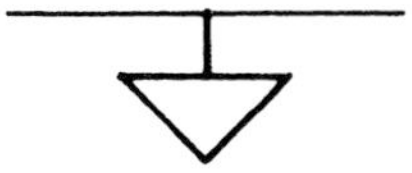

Alarm call point

Sprinkler

Visual warning device

Smoke detector

Audible warning device

Heat detector

Indicator panel

Non-active lines and symbols

Coordinating
dimension

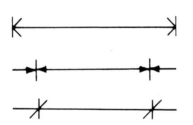

Other dimensions generally. The method, although recommended in most BSI literature, tends to be replaced in practice by the oblique slashes shown below. Most commonly used method for general dimensioning. Neat, legible and rapid

Controlling line

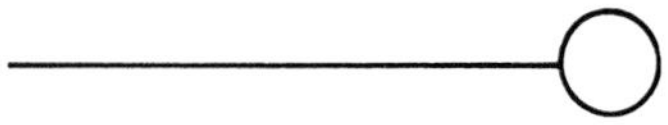

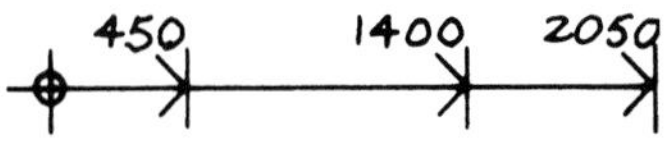

Running dimensions. Use should be restricted to surveys

Small dimensions are best indicated thus

Modular dimension

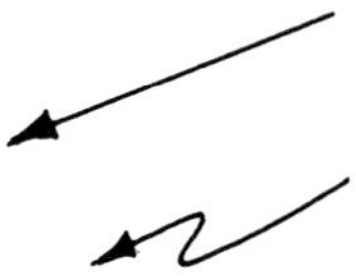

Leader lines, indicating where notes or descriptions apply

Centre lines or grid lines.
Drawn in thin line to distinguish them from service runs.
(See Appendix 1)

Dotted line indicates important lines hidden in the particular plan or section view taken. (Also, on demolition drawings, work to be removed)

Break line

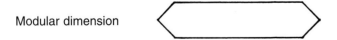

Section line. The arrows point in the direction of view and the line joining them indicates the plane of the section

Spot level—existing $\times$ 27.305

Spot level—proposed $\times$ |27.305|

27.305
▽

Level shown on section or elevation—existing

|27.305|
▽

Level shown on section or elevation—proposed

Some abbreviations in common use

AD	above datum
app.	approximately
BM	bench mark
BSCP	British Standard Code of Practice
BSS	British Standard Specification
c/c	centre to centre
₵	centre line
diam.	diameter
dim.	dimension
exc.	excavate (excavation)
exg.	existing
Eq.	equal
extn.	extension
FFL	finished floor level
fin.	finish (finished)
FS	full size
fluor.	fluorescent
HD	heavy duty

HT	high tension
Htg.	heating
H/V (or H & V)	heating and ventilation
ID	internal diameter
inc.	including (inclusive)
int.	internal (interior)
IV	invert
LT	low tension
max.	maximum
mfr.	manufacturer
min.	minimum
misc.	miscellaneous
NBS	National Building Specification
nom.	nominal
NTS	not to scale
o/a	overall
OD	outside diameter
O/H	overhead
opp.	opposite
partn.	partition
PC	pre-cast
pr.	pair
prefab.	pre-fabricated
pt.	point (or part, depending on context)
rect.	rectangular (rectilinear)
reinf.	reinforced
rad.	radius
req.	required
ret.	return (returned)
sch.	schedule
spec.	specification
susp.	suspended
sq.	square
std.	standard
vert.	vertical
wt.	weight

Glossary of CAD terms

Architectural CAD packages or programs

(Based on AutoCAD terminology. Other programs may use different terms.)

These are CAD programs with capabilities beyond the drawing of simple lines, arcs and text. They have additional capabilities specific to the architectural and building industries and usually allow a 3D model of the building to be created from intelligent 'objects' rather than simple entities.

Attribute   A special type of text entity, included within a block definition that can be used to hold information about that block. Attribute information can be defined, set and read by the CAD program, making automated links to separate databases possible.

Blocks   A set of entities defined so that they act as if they were a single entity. For example, a WC is drawn with a few lines and an arc and saved to disk as a separate drawing. It is then 'inserted' into plans as many times as is needed. Generally blocks are inserted full size (1:1).

CAD and CADD   'Computer-Aided Draughting', 'Computer-Aided Design', and 'Computer-Aided Design and Draughting' are terms that refer to the process of creating drawings or designing with the aid of computers.

Database   An organised collection of data that can be interpreted and operated upon by a computer. A drawing file is effectively a database of drawn information that is manipulated by a CAD program. CAD users also refer to 'External Databases'. These refer to data files other than the drawing file.

Dimension entities   Dimensions that are calculated by the program based on the entities to which they are attached. Most CAD users use 'associative' dimensions that update automatically when the entity that the dimension relates to is modified. Non-associative dimensions require the CAD user to type in the dimension text manually and their use can be dangerous.

Drawing (1)   A drawing in the conventionally understood sense, printed or plotted on to paper, and created from the CAD file.

Drawing (2)   Sometimes called the 'Model File'. A computer file containing the 'model' information describing all or part of a building, plus definitions of any number of paper plots that might be created from it. This was not always so. Early versions of CAD programs could only create small files, containing just one plotted drawing. When CAD terminology was being coined, it wasn't important to distinguish between the paper plot and the computer file used to generate it. The name stuck, hence the current confusion.

Dyeline machine   A machine used for preparing paper prints from large drawings. Now largely superseded by large format photocopiers. Many CAD users now create multiple 'originals' rather than one original from which copies are made.

DXF   As in filename.dxf. A common file format used for the transfer of files from one CAD system to another. All major CAD systems can convert between their own native file format and DXF.

DWG   As in filename.dwg. AutoCAD's file format. Because AutoCAD is so widely used, many other CAD programs can read and write direct to AutoCAD format, though often with inconsistent results.

DGN   As in filename.dgn. Microstation's file format. Microstation is another widely used CAD program.

Entities   Arcs, lines, circles, text, faces and so on, held in the drawing file, together with information about their size, position and orientation. In dedicated architectural design programs, walls, windows, and so on might also be defined as 'entities'.

Internet   A communications network linking computers, that allows people to share information. Now used extensively to obtain information from manufacturers, to order goods, as a means of communication by email, and for transfer of CAD and other computer files between professionals.

Layers   May be known as 'levels' in some CAD programs. A way of grouping entities together so that their visibility can be controlled as a named set. The CAD version of 'Overlay Draughting'.

Model, CAD model   The set of entities, objects and other data that describe the project in full in 2D or 3D. This is the data set from which the paper drawings are created.

Objects   Some dedicated architectural CAD programs create their drawings from 'intelligent objects' rather than entities. CAD files will be created from doors, walls and windows rather than lines, arcs and circles. A 'door' object knows it is a door and interacts appropriately with a 'wall' object. Move the door, say, and the adjacent light switch moves with it. Flip the door and the light switch moves to the other side without intervention by the designer.

Pin registration (overlay draughting)   A manual drawing method that enjoyed popularity in a few offices before the advent of CAD. Each type of information was drawn on a different sheet of acetate, say walls on one sheet, doors on a second and light fittings on a third. Sheets were aligned by dropping the appropriate sheets over pins fixed in the drawing board. Once the individual sheets were finished different paper drawings could be created by photographing the combined image.

Printing and plotting   The distinction between printing and plotting is less important than it once was. In the early days of CAD, the only machines capable of producing large format architectural drawings accurately to scale were pen and drum plotters. Printers, on the other hand, were slow, low resolution devices, printing mostly to A4 size.

Today, large format pen plotters have largely been abandoned as expensive and as too troublesome to maintain. They have been replaced by reliable, large format inkjet 'plotters' which use the same technology as A4 inkjet printers.

Daisy-wheel and dot-matrix printers have now been replaced with high resolution laser and inkjet printers, equally capable of producing text documents, colour photographs, 3D photo-realistic images and drawings. The terms 'printing' and 'plotting' now refer as much to size as to printing method. The terms are becoming interchangeable in common usage.

Symbols   A set of symbols designed so that they act as if they were a single entity in the same way a block is defined. For example, the symbol for a light fitting. Like blocks, they are then 'inserted' into plans as many times as is needed. Generally, symbols can be inserted at any scale, to make them bigger or smaller on the plotted drawing.

Index

Index